OKANAGAN COLLEGE LIBRARY

04449740

D0753304

EYEWITNESS ● ART

MONET

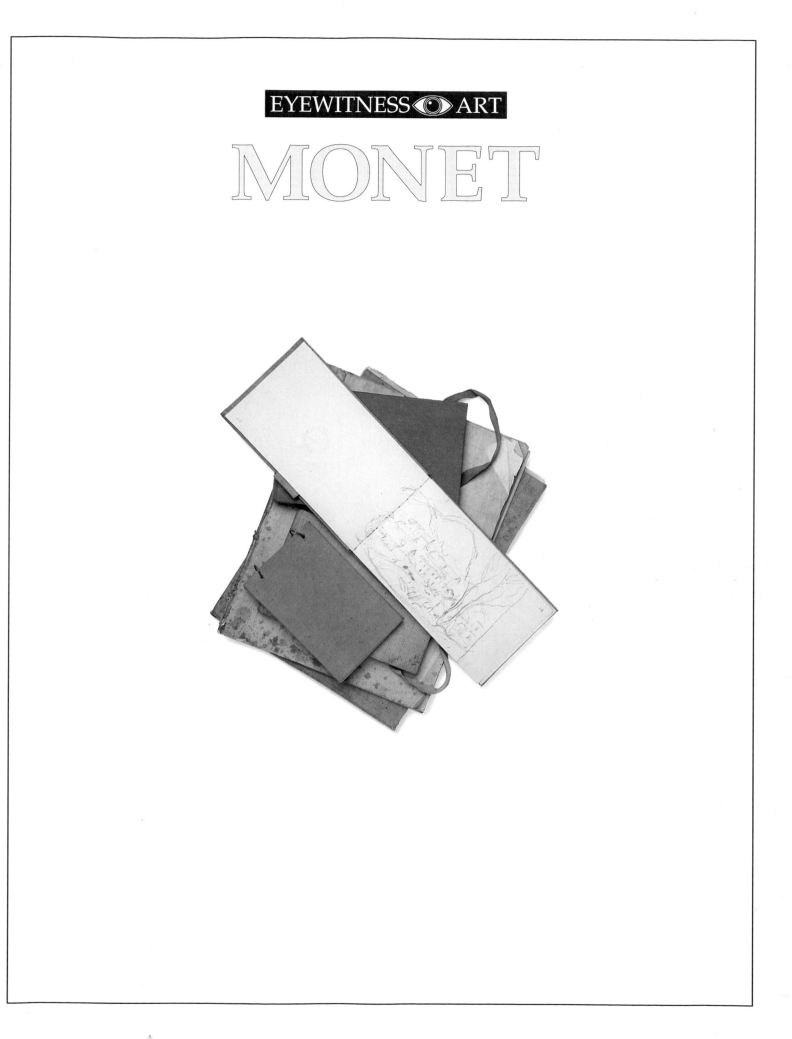

Wild Coast, Belle-Ile (1886)

Monet in his studio
with *Waterlilies* canvases

Woman with a Parasol (1886)

Sketchbook with
drawings of
Rouen Cathedral

Monet's
floating studio

OKANAGAN COLLEGE
LIBRARY
BRITISH COLUMBIA

EYEWITNESS ART

MONET

JUDE WELTON

Volume from
Monet's botanical library

Letter to
a patron

Sketch of an iris

Pencil sketch of
one of Monet's sons

Monet's quill pen

Letter opener
belonging
to Monet

DK

DORLING KINDERSLEY
London • New York • Stuttgart
in association with
THE MUSÉE MARMOTTAN, PARIS

Waterlily from
the garden at Giverny

Monet's
palette

Monet in his garden

Painting
umbrella

A DORLING KINDERSLEY BOOK

To my Gran, Sarah Anne Spedding

Project editor Laura Harper
Art editor Tracy Hambleton
Series editor Gwen Edmonds
Series art editor Toni Rann
Editorial and visual researcher Julia Harris-Voss
Design assistant Claire Pegrum
Managing editor Sean Moore
Managing art editor Tina Vaughan
DTP manager Joanna Figg-Latham
DTP designer Doug Miller
Production controller Meryl Silbert

This Eyewitness ®/™ Art book
first published in Great Britain in 1992 by
Dorling Kindersley Limited,
9 Henrietta Street, London WC2E 8PS

Copyright © 1992 Dorling Kindersley Limited

All rights reserved. No part of this publication
may be reproduced, stored in a retrieval system,
or transmitted in any form or by any means,
electronic, mechanical, photocopying, recording
or otherwise, without the prior written
permission of the copyright owner.

A CIP catalogue record for this book is
available from the British Library

ISBN 0 86318 932 6

Colour reproduction by
GRB Editrice s.r.l.
Printed in Italy by
A. Mondadori Editore, Verona

Studio easel

One of Monet's paintbrushes

Contents

From coast to capital

Le Havre – the Grand Quai

"I WAS BORN IN PARIS IN 1840 ... in an environment entirely concerned with commerce, where everyone professed a contemptuous disdain for art. But my youth was passed at Le Havre...." This is how Monet began telling his life story to an interviewer in 1900. From early on, he had an aversion towards formal education, but he showed a natural talent for caricature and made a good living as a teenager, selling portraits to the citizens of Le Havre. A local landscape artist, Eugène Boudin, persuaded Monet to join him in open-air painting sessions on the coast. "Suddenly a veil was torn away," Monet declared, "my destiny as a painter opened up to me". Despite his father's reluctance, he was eventually allowed to go to Paris to study art. In 1861, he was conscripted into the army and posted to Algeria. But in 1862, he was back in Paris, determined to make his mark as an independent artist.

Teenage caricatures

The young Monet gained a reputation for his caricatures, which were exhibited in an art materials shop in Le Havre. They impressed Boudin, whose work was displayed in the same shop.

COMMISSIONED PORTRAIT *left*
Monet gained his first income from local sitters, such as this unidentified woman. They paid 20 francs for their portrait and the money helped to finance his stay in Paris.

NEWSPAPER EDITOR
Many of Monet's caricatures were based on images he found in magazines. This one, taken from a photograph by Nadar, shows editor, Jules de Prémaray, holding his newspaper (*La Patrie*) like a flag.

BOUDIN BY MONET
Boudin owned a framing shop in Le Havre, and visiting artists, such as Jean-François Millet and Constant Troyon, had encouraged him to paint. Though his oil paintings were timid and small-scale (p. 17), they were executed entirely in the open air and, as such, were radically different from most contemporary works. The young Monet hated them at first, but in time the gentle, generous Boudin became his mentor.

THE ARTIST AS A YOUNG MAN
This photograph shows Monet in his early twenties, looking a little dandified and very self-confident – traits for which he was to be noted all his life. "Without my dear Monet, who gave us all courage, we would have given up!" Auguste Renoir was to recall. Even during Monet's first visit to Paris, he defiantly rejected "official" art and interested himself only in "experimenters".

MODERN PARIS
The Paris in which the 19-year-old Monet arrived in 1859 had recently been transformed by the architect, Baron Haussmann, from a medieval city to a modern metropolis. It was the undisputed capital of artistic activity, both traditional and avant-garde. Despite instructions from his family and advice from friends, Monet did not follow convention and study "academic" painting. Instead, he opted for the Atelier Suisse, an independent studio where he could attend life classes without formal tuition. It was there that he met Camille Pissarro, who was to become a fellow Impressionist.

TERRACE AT SAINTE-ADRESSE
1867; 98 x 130 cm (38½ x 51 in)
Painted at the family home near Le Havre, this picture gives a clear idea of Monet's middle-class background. The seated man is his father. The woman beside him – whose head the artist has daringly obscured with a parasol – is Monet's aunt, Madame Lecadre. (His mother had died in 1857.) Presumably it is his cousin who stands talking to a gentleman friend, both of them silhouetted against the sea. Monet's father worked in the family's wholesale grocery and ships' chandlers, and was suspicious of his son's artistic ambitions. It was probably thanks to Madame Lecadre – an amateur painter – that the young artist was allowed to go to Paris at all.

MONET IN UNIFORM
Monet was sent to Algeria in the *Chasseurs d'Afrique* regiment. Later he said: "The impressions of colour and light that I received there contained the germ of my future researches".

THE MUSEUM AT LE HAVRE
1873; 75 x 100 cm (29½ x 39 in)
Monet never lost touch with Le Havre, and the Normandy coast in general remained a source of inspiration throughout his life. After he was invalided out of the army with typhoid in 1861, he spent his convalescence painting in and around Le Havre. It was then that he met, and worked with, the Dutch artist, Johan-Barthold Jongkind, whose atmospheric marine pictures he already admired. Monet later said: "To him, I owe the final education of my eye".

Portrait of Monet in Algerian uniform by Charles Lhuillier, 1861

The artist's studio

"MY STUDIO! But I have never had a studio," Monet declared in an interview almost 20 years after he painted the picture opposite. With a grandiose sweep of his arm, indicating the surrounding countryside, he continued, "That is my studio". One of the myths linked to Monet – and one that he liked to perpetuate – is that his paintings were executed entirely out of doors. Undoubtedly, his direct response to nature was the essence of his art, but he always had access to some kind of studio. In the 1860s, he constructed ambitious figure paintings indoors, having first made sketches in the open air (pp. 12–13). Studio work, on pictures he had started outside, became increasingly important to him after the decade of "pure Impressionism" – the 1870s. The huge waterlily decorations (pp. 60–61), for example, which occupied his final years, were executed entirely in a large studio that was specially constructed to accommodate them.

MONET'S PALETTE
Monet used this palette when he was an old man; it shows the colours he was using then – lighter than those employed opposite. From the mid-1860s onwards, he worked with a limited range of bright, pure pigments, often mixed with white. At the centre of the palette is cobalt blue, a pigment he favoured throughout his career.

The Corner of the Studio

1861; 182 x 127 cm (72 x 50 in)
This large painting, with its sombre colours, tonal modelling, and black shadows, appears far removed from what most people associate with Monet. But its unidealized approach shows the 20-year-old artist already rejecting the immaculately finished classicism of academic painting in favour of the Realism that was expounded by Gustave Courbet.

STUDIO EASEL
This is one of several large studio easels still remaining at Monet's final home at Giverny (pp. 34–35).

Handle with which to raise or lower easel

Small ring-bound book containing only one sketch (p. 49)

The sketchbooks are in varying states of repair. This large book has no cover

Sketched here are the angle of a quay and the grouping of boats and figures

These lines may suggest a potential crop

MONET'S SKETCHBOOKS
Despite his early caricatures, detailed drawing played no role in Monet's working method in his later life. However, his surviving sketchbooks show that he used rough sketches from the 1860s until the 1920s. Apparently, he did not consider them as works of art in any way; for example, sometimes he even drew one sketch over another. He saw them as preliminary notes, made while he searched for his motif, experimenting with viewpoints and trying out various different ways of positioning elements on the page. The sketchbooks range in size from 9 x 14.5 cm (3½ x 6 in) to 26 x 34 cm (10 x 13 in).

INTERIOR DESIGN

The heavily patterned wallpaper and carpet indicate that this is not a studio as such, but the room of an artist. The traditional studios that were used by academic painters had dark walls, helping to create deep shadows; the Impressionists preferred light-filled studios painted with pale colours.

PAINTER'S PROPS

Familiar still-life props hang above the table and lean against it – a sword, a pistol, and a rifle. A pile of well-thumbed books adds a serious air, and a tasselled velvet cap has been draped, with studied casualness, over the table edge. More obvious artist's accoutrements are the box of paints, and the loaded palette with several brushes.

SHADOW PLAY

The rounded surfaces of the turned table legs have been modelled with light and shade. Monet has created dark shadows that move through mid-tones to white highlights. Within a few years, he would have begun to use colour to describe form. He virtually eliminated black from his pictures, even in the shadows. The violet shadows in *Red Boats* (pp. 22–23), make a good comparison.

9

Painting in the forest

Monet's family bought him out of the army (pp. 6–7) on condition that he continue his artistic studies in Paris with a recognized teacher. In 1862, the headstrong young artist grudgingly joined the studio of Charles Gleyre, where he was outraged by the master's criticism of his painting as being too true to nature and not close enough to the ideals of classical beauty. But he met some kindred spirits at the studio – Frédéric Bazille, Alfred Sisley, and Auguste Renoir – and persuaded them to join him on painting trips to the Forest of Fontainebleau outside Paris. Landscape painters such as Charles-François Daubigny and Camille Corot had been practising *plein air* (open-air) painting there for some years.

ALDERS
Charles-François Daubigny; 1872; 33 x 57 cm (13 x 22½ in); oil on wood
Daubigny was one of the "Barbizon" painters, who frequented the village of that name in the Forest of Fontainebleau. While landscapes such as this were admired for their truth to nature, some were criticized for being only "an impression".

WORKING OUTDOORS
Corot at work in the open air in 1871. The painting umbrella helped to control the amount of light falling on the canvas.

THE LEANING TREE TRUNK
Camille Corot; c.1865; 50 x 61 cm (19¾ x 24 in)
Corot based soft-edged landscapes such as this on his observations of nature, but reworked them in the studio. Monet later described him as the "greatest landscape painter" of all.

THE ROAD FROM CHAILLY
1865; 42 x 59 cm (16½ x 23 in)
Monet spent the spring and summer of 1865 staying in the village of Chailly-en-Bière, in the Forest of Fontainebleau. He was already dedicated to the idea of painting in the open air, as he had been taught by Johan-Barthold Jongkind and Eugène Boudin (pp. 6–7). Gleyre's studio had closed down in 1864, and two of Monet's fellow students, Renoir and Sisley, were also working in the Forest, based at Marlotte. In this woodland scene near Chailly, as in many of his early landscapes, Monet has used the diagonal of a receding road to create a powerful sense of depth. He may have intended to use such a composition as the basis for his large-scale *Le Déjeuner sur l'Herbe* (pp. 12–13), but as the picture evolved, he closed up the deep perspective and surrounded his figures with trees.

TRAVELLING EASEL
The *chevelet de campagne*, literally "country easel", was an essential part of an open-air painter's equipment.

Portable materials

The invention of collapsible metal tubes of paint in the 1840s made oil painting out of doors really viable for the first time. As *plein air* painting increased in popularity, an industry grew up that provided artists with portable equipment – from folding easels to conveniently small-scale canvases. Most landscape artists still considered their open-air paintings as sketches, or studies, which would form the basis of studio compositions.

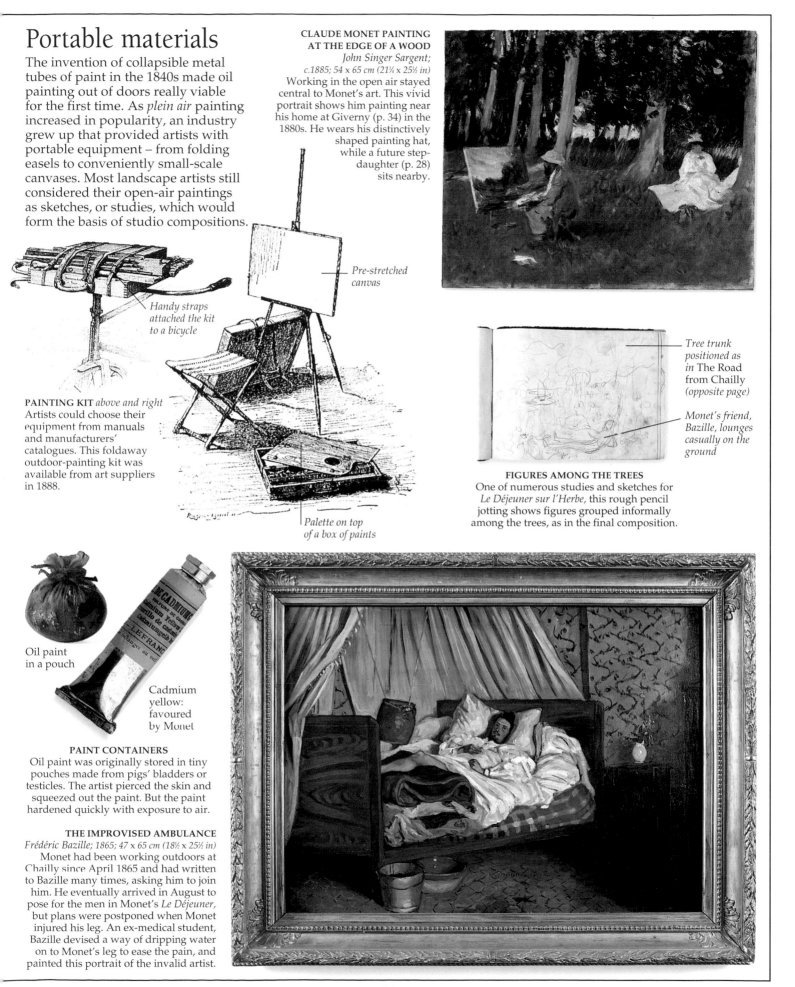

CLAUDE MONET PAINTING AT THE EDGE OF A WOOD
John Singer Sargent;
c.1885; 54 x 65 cm (21¼ x 25½ in)
Working in the open air stayed central to Monet's art. This vivid portrait shows him painting near his home at Giverny (p. 34) in the 1880s. He wears his distinctively shaped painting hat, while a future step-daughter (p. 28) sits nearby.

Pre-stretched canvas

Handy straps attached the kit to a bicycle

PAINTING KIT *above and right*
Artists could choose their equipment from manuals and manufacturers' catalogues. This foldaway outdoor-painting kit was available from art suppliers in 1888.

Palette on top of a box of paints

Tree trunk positioned as in The Road from Chailly *(opposite page)*

Monet's friend, Bazille, lounges casually on the ground

FIGURES AMONG THE TREES
One of numerous studies and sketches for *Le Déjeuner sur l'Herbe*, this rough pencil jotting shows figures grouped informally among the trees, as in the final composition.

Oil paint in a pouch

Cadmium yellow: favoured by Monet

PAINT CONTAINERS
Oil paint was originally stored in tiny pouches made from pigs' bladders or testicles. The artist pierced the skin and squeezed out the paint. But the paint hardened quickly with exposure to air.

THE IMPROVISED AMBULANCE
Frédéric Bazille; 1865; 47 x 65 cm (18½ x 25½ in)
Monet had been working outdoors at Chailly since April 1865 and had written to Bazille many times, asking him to join him. He eventually arrived in August to pose for the men in Monet's *Le Déjeuner*, but plans were postponed when Monet injured his leg. An ex-medical student, Bazille devised a way of dripping water on to Monet's leg to ease the pain, and painted this portrait of the invalid artist.

11

Challenging Manet

THE MOST AMBITIOUS PAINTING of Monet's early
years was never completed and is now reduced
to fragments. The artist gave it to a landlord in
lieu of rent, and it was rolled up and left to rot.
Monet had planned a huge composition, with
12 life-size figures enjoying a picnic in a glade,
and intended to submit it to the 1866 Salon –
France's official annual painting exhibition. The
scale of the work reflects his determination to
get noticed, and it is likely that his choice of
subject represents a challenge to Edouard Manet's
Le Déjeuner (below), which had attracted a great
deal of scandalized attention in 1863. But the two
works are significantly different: Monet's contains
neither art-historical references nor the ironic
pairing of naked women with overdressed
dandies. It simply shows an ordinary middle-
class picnic, painted with natural light effects.
Monet was obsessed with the project, but missed
the Salon deadline, and abandoned it in 1866.

LE DEJEUNER SUR L'HERBE
Edouard Manet; 1863; 2 m 8 cm x 2 m 64 cm (6 ft 8¼ in x 8 ft 6½ in)
Respect and rivalry mingled in Monet's attitude towards Manet, who had
succeeded Gustave Courbet as the unofficial leader of avant-garde artists.
Manet had been the centre of attention in 1863, when this painting was
shown at the Salon des Refusés – the alternative exhibition venue for artists
rejected by the Salon. People recognized the work's similarity to a celebrated
Renaissance painting thought to be by the Venetian master, Giorgione (since
re-attributed to Titian), but were offended by the "indecency" of depicting
a nude woman with two men in modern dress. As in Monet's later version,
the figures are painted life-size in a landscape setting, but the references to
Old Masters and the studio lighting emphasize the artificiality of picture-
making. Monet encouraged Manet to paint in the open air when the two
artists worked together at Argenteuil in 1874 (p. 22).

Le Déjeuner sur l'Herbe

1866; left and central fragments; left: 4 m 18 cm x 1 m 50 cm
(13 ft 7 in x 4 ft 9 in); central: 2 m 48 cm x 2 m 17 cm (8 ft 1¼ in x 7 ft 1¼ in)

In the l9th century, only historical, mythological, or biblical subjects were usually considered worthy of being painted on such a monumental scale. Courbet had already caused shock waves in the art world by presenting massive images that featured life-size portraits of working-class country folk. And here Monet has used the huge size of the canvas to elevate a leisurely bourgeois scene to the status of history painting. The casualness of the composition has much in common with the informal group photographs that were becoming popular at the time. Its contemporary theme reflects an influential essay – "The Painter of Modern Life"– by the poet, Charles Baudelaire, in which he called upon artists to reflect "the heroism of modern life" in their works.

FINAL OIL STUDY *above*
As Monet told the art collector, the Duc de Trévise, "I proceeded how everyone did then, bit by bit with studies from nature, which I put together in my studio". After months of preliminary sketches, he spent the autumn of 1865 working on this final study. It measures 130 x 181 cm (51 x 71¼ in) – about a third of the size of the full-scale picture.

A TREASURED FRAGMENT
When the Duc de Trévise visited Monet in 1920 (above), the 80-year-old artist paused in front of *Le Déjeuner* and told him: "It is very dear to me, this piece, even though it is incomplete and mutilated".

PORTRAIT OF COURBET?
In the full-scale painting, Monet replaced the seated young man from the oil study with a rotund, bearded figure strongly resembling Gustave Courbet, whose swaggering persona and distinctive features are caricatured here. According to some sources, it may have been Courbet's criticisms that led Monet to abandon *Le Déjeuner*.

CHANGING FASHIONS *left*
As the left-hand fragment shows, fashion had changed since Monet completed his final oil study (top right). He has given one of the female figures a more up-to-the-minute hat and shortened the hemlines on both the dresses by obliterating part of the original trailing skirts with shadows. All the women in the painting were modelled by Monet's new girlfriend, Camille Doncieux.

BOLD HIGHLIGHTS *above*
The slab-like highlights of pale blue and white on the figures and cloth show the boldness of Monet's technique. Although the highlights suggest forms, they also create a surface pattern of flat colour. Always concerned with both depth and surface in his paintings, Monet remained particularly attached to this early, ambitious attempt to reconcile these two aspects.

Poverty and progress

Paris fashion
plate, c.1868

In 1866, having abandoned *Le Déjeuner* (pp. 12–13), Monet rapidly painted a life-size picture of Camille (p. 25), which became one of the most talked-about paintings at the Salon that year. But this taste of success and the welcome (though temporary) resumption of his parental allowance were followed by years of dire poverty, during which he relied on financial aid from fellow artists. At one stage, he claimed that he had tried to drown himself, though he may have been exaggerating to add weight to a begging letter he sent to Bazille. Despite Monet's poverty, the 1860s saw striking developments in his art, as he and his friends evolved a new way of painting their world.

FASHIONABLE SOURCES
Monet seems to have referred to fashion plates not only for the clothes but also for poses and groupings.

SUNLIT FABRIC
The pale fabrics of dresses worn during the late 1860s had pure colours and light-reflecting qualities that Monet appreciated. At the same time, they provided his paintings with an aspect of modernity.

A PASSION FOR PARASOLS
Parasols, favourite fashion accessories in Monet's day, appear repeatedly in his pictures of women. His fellow painter, Berthe Morisot, noted that when Monet was around "one knew which way to turn one's parasol".

WOMEN IN THE GARDEN
1866; 256 x 208 cm (100¾ x 82 in)
Learning from the problems he had encountered in *Le Déjeuner*, Monet determined to execute a life-size figure painting entirely out of doors. He dug a trench in the garden of the house that he had rented at Ville d'Avray, into which he could lower his canvas to help him reach the top section. Camille, wearing in turn the same dresses as she had worn in *Le Déjeuner*, posed for all the figures. Gustave Courbet visited Monet while he was at work on this picture in 1866, and was surprised to find him waiting until the light was right to paint the leaves. The idyllic atmosphere of the work gives no hint of Monet's financial straits at that time: he fled the house in late summer, after slashing 200 canvases in a failed attempt to keep them from his creditors.

BATHERS AT LA GRENOUILLERE
1869; 73 x 92 cm (28¾ x 36¼ in)
The riverside scene shown in this picture suited Monet's taste in subject matter, combining an informal view of contemporary leisure with the fleeting effects of sunlight on water. Though Monet was to dismiss this as a "bad *pochade*" ("bad sketch"), it is one of his most significant early works, in which he developed his own distinctive style. Painted rapidly on the spot, in vigorous, individual dashes of bright colour, it brilliantly captures the impression of bustling activity in an open-air setting. The long, wooden pier boldly cuts the painting in half.

THE BATHERS IN DETAIL
Behind the costume-clad bathers are swimmers who, like the water, are daringly and rather crudely reduced to individual slabs of paint.

Side-by-side with Renoir

Monet spent the summer of 1869 near Bougival, outside Paris, in such hardship that Auguste Renoir, who was staying nearby, would bring him and Camille scraps of food. But as the two artists painted beside each other at the bathing resort of La Grenouillère, Monet produced works of striking originality.

LA GRENOUILLERE
Auguste Renoir; 1869; 65 x 93 cm (25½ x 36½ in)
Despite the similarities with Monet's image, this differs in technique and approach: the brushwork is feathery and the primary interest is in the people.

LETTER TO A FRIEND
In January 1869, Monet ran out of money and paint. In this letter to Bazille, he asks for paints, specifying plenty of white, black, and cobalt blue.

BAZILLE'S STUDIO
Frédéric Bazille; 1870; 98 x 128.5 cm (38½ x 50½ in)
When in Paris, Monet mixed with artists who shared his contempt for official art. Here he stands to the left of Edouard Manet, who is facing the easel, with Bazille on the right.

SELF-PORTRAIT WITH PALETTE
Frédéric Bazille; 1865;
108.5 x 72.5 cm (42¾ x 28½ in)
A generous friend, Bazille shared his studio with Monet and Renoir, and bought *Women in the Garden*.

Open-air impressions

PAINTED AT A SINGLE SITTING in the open air, on a small, portable canvas, the picture below is one of the most vivid examples of what was to become known as Impressionism. The simplified forms, broad brushstrokes, and the startling composition create a sense of immediacy, which is accentuated by an unintentional addition to the picture – a sea-breeze blew sand on to the canvas, embedding it in the wet paint. Despite the painting's lack of traditional finish, the fact that Monet dated and initialled the canvas suggests that he considered it complete.

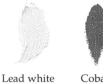 

Lead white   Cobalt blue   Ultramarine

Ivory black   Viridian   Vermilion   Red-brown ochre   Yellow ochre

ARTIST'S PALETTE
Technical analysis has identified the pigments above, and the paint media as both poppy oil and linseed oil. Poppy oil, which dries more slowly and yellows less with age than linseed oil, was found in the white *impasto* (thickly applied) highlights.

GREY GROUND
The pale grey ground has rubbed off in one corner of the canvas.

SAND PARTICLES
This thickly painted highlight on the dress of the left-hand figure is peppered with sand.

SHADY PARASOL
The blue of Camille's parasol has been roughly scrubbed in with thinned paint, leaving areas of grey ground showing through, sometimes completely uncovered. There is no modelling to suggest the parasol's domed shape. Using a narrow brush, Monet drew in the spokes and edges in black, and dragged in the brown line of the handle. A single thick stroke of white depicts the highlighted outer surface.

Two patches of pinky brown and a few flicks of black suffice to indicate the facial features

The cobalt blue bow stands out brilliantly between the white collar and the black dress

WOMAN IN BLACK
Although this painting shows close-up views of two women, Monet has not treated his figures as "portraits" that have individualized features. However, he has captured the quiet concentration on this woman's face with a caricaturist's economy. Her dress and hat are not pure black – a colour rarely found in Impressionist painting – instead, they consist of ivory black mixed with vermilion, earth colours, and cobalt blue.

WET-IN-WET *left*
Completing a painting at a single session, as Monet did here, means that there is no time for a layer of oil paint to dry. The artist worked wet-in-wet, applying one colour of paint next to, and over another that was still wet. This detail of Camille's bonnet shows how Monet used dabs of yellow, blue, and red, and streaks of green, mixing some of the pigments as he did so.

Though colours have intermingled in places, individual brushmarks remain distinct

The Beach at Trouville
1870; 37.5 x 46 cm (14¾ x 18 in)

Monet has chosen such a close-up view that the woman on the right is cropped off by the edge of the canvas. She may be a relative of Monet's, or Madame Boudin. Camille sits on the left, and little Jean's shoe hangs on the chair between the women.

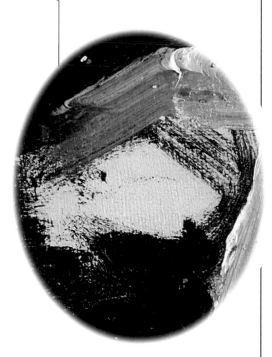

NEGATIVE IMAGES
One of the most audacious aspects of the painting is the way Monet has suggested a hand simply by leaving the pale ground to stand out as a highlight within the area of the black dress. For the newspaper, Monet has used a square-ended brush, as he did for the thick slabs of white on Camille's lap. Here the black underpainting shows through and mixes with the white.

Argenteuil days

THE FIRST HOUSE
In 1871, Monet rented this house near the railway for 1,000 francs a year.

THE RIVERSIDE SUBURB of Argenteuil, only a 15-minute train ride from Paris, was popular for day trips and weekend sailing. The years that Monet spent there, 1871–1878, were the most settled and prolific in the first half of his life. He produced more than 170 works at Argenteuil – images of his wife and son in their garden or in nearby meadows, and a huge number of local river scenes. Despite his complaints of poverty, he enjoyed a comfortable lifestyle, initially supported by Paul Durand-Ruel, the art dealer he had met in London in 1870. Between 1872 and 1873, Durand-Ruel spent 29,000 francs on Monet's paintings. But when the dealer stopped buying for a few years because of his own financial difficulties, Monet continued to live beyond his means, and requests for loans from friends and patrons persisted.

THE SECOND HOUSE
In 1874, the Monet family moved around the corner to a larger house.

THE LUNCHEON
1873; 162 x 203 cm (63¾ x 80 in)
Monet painted this large canvas while still at the first house. It is an inviting yet wistful image. Little Jean sits alone in the dappled shadows, absorbed in his toys; Camille and an unidentified woman are walking in the background. The bonnet that hangs from a branch accentuates the decorative qualities of the painting.

A 1990 replica of Monet's floating studio

THE FLOATING STUDIO
Following the example of the painter, Charles-François Daubigny, Monet had a studio boat built. It had a cabin large enough for him to sit inside and paint, but he could also work outside on the open deck, protected by a canvas canopy. Unlike Daubigny, who had made long painting trips in his boat, Monet stayed close to home, mooring his floating studio on a quiet stretch of the Seine or in the midst of the bustling activity of the popular sailing areas.

CLAUDE MONET READING
Auguste Renoir; 1872;
61 x 50 cm (24 x 19½ in)
Whilst at Argenteuil, Monet often played host to his artist friends, including Manet, Renoir, and Sisley. Manet lived nearby; it was he who had found Monet his first house there. Renoir painted this portrait of Monet during one visit. Rather than depicting his friend as an artist, as he sometimes did (p. 25), Renoir shows him in a homely pose with pipe and newspaper.

MONET'S PIPE
A habitual smoker, Monet was often pictured with a cigarette when working. This is one of the pipes he would smoke when relaxing.

SAILING COMPETITIONS *left*
Argenteuil held its first regatta in 1850, and by 1871, when Monet arrived, this section of the Seine had become such a prime site for sailing that the suburb had even hosted international competitions. Argenteuil's association with boating was one of its main attractions for Monet; the numerous leisure boats there were a constant source of inspiration for him.

Argenteuil regatta poster

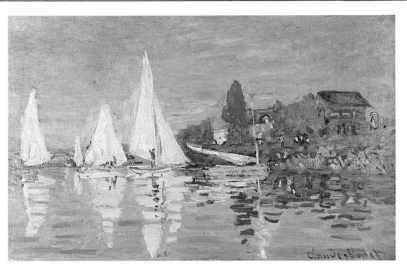

BOATS; REGATTA AT ARGENTEUIL
1872; 48 x 75 cm (19 x 30 in)
This bold little painting may be the rapid sketch that Monet sold to his neighbour and fellow painter, Gustave Caillebotte. To capture fleeting effects of light on water, Monet painted the reflections with slabs of cream, blue, orange, red, and green. He did not blend the brushstrokes as in a traditionally "finished" painting: the *taches* – patches of colour – have a hard-edged clarity.

LETTER TO A PATRON *below*
One of Monet's most loyal collectors during his years at Argenteuil was the local homoeopathic doctor, Georges de Bellio. Two days before Monet's intended departure from Argenteuil, in January 1878, he wrote to ask – or rather beg – the doctor for 200 francs to help him pay his outstanding debts: "You have done so much to bail me out during the past two years that I hope you wouldn't want to abandon me just as I am reaching dry land".

A fabric sun canopy could be rolled up when the studio was not in use

Windows line the front, back, and side walls of the cabin

Sharply pointed prow constructed to a local traditional design

BRIDGE OVER THE RIVER SEINE
Two bridges crossed the Seine at Argenteuil when Monet lived there – a railway bridge and a road bridge (right). Both were under repair when he first arrived, as they had been damaged during the Franco-Prussian war. They feature in many of his paintings.

Painting on the Seine

MONET PAINTED THE SAILING BOATS at Argenteuil (p. 20) many times – either setting up his easel on the riverbank, or working in his floating studio (below), as he did for the composition opposite. Although he painted such scenes directly, he did not simply depict whatever happened to be in front of him, but always constructed his pictures deliberately. This painting is consciously influenced by Japanese prints. Despite the growing industrialization of Argenteuil, Monet has presented a scene of unspoiled calm by "editing out" the factory chimneys that would have been visible on the horizon.

JAPANESE INSPIRATION
This print of *Tsukuda Beneath a Full Moon*, by Ando Hiroshige, is one of dozens of Japanese prints in Monet's personal collection. Monet and his Impressionist friends were inspired by the way Japanese artists used bold, flat areas of colour and emphasized the picture plane. By cropping off the masts of his boats, Hiroshige has effectively tied them to the picture plane – a device that influenced many of Monet's works.

MONET IN HIS FLOATING STUDIO
Edouard Manet; 1874; 80 x 98 cm (31½ x 38½ in)
Manet has painted his friend working in his floating studio in the boat-rental area at Argenteuil. Despite his complaints about lack of funds, Monet is dressed as a well-to-do, bourgeois painter. His first wife, Camille, sits at the cabin doorway. The boat-rental house is visible on the left bank, as in Monet's *Red Boats* (opposite). But unlike his fellow artist, Manet has included the factory chimneys, potent symbols of "modern life" – a theme that was central to his art.

BENEATH THE CANOPY
This sketch by Monet, which was made while his studio was moored in the boat-rental area, gives a vivid impression of the artist at work and shows how close he was to his subject. A figure – probably Camille – is seated in front of him and has been lightly sketched in.

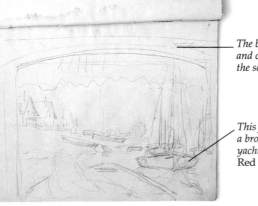

The boat's doorway and canopy frame the scene

This front view of a broad-bottomed yacht is used in Red Boats

Red Boats

c.1875; 55 x 65 cm (21½ x 25½ in)
This is one of several paintings Monet made at Argenteuil's boat-rental area, where weekend sailors hired yachts by the hour. Many of his works show side views of yachts in full sail, but this tranquil scene features a front view of the moored, bare-masted boats.

PARALLEL LINES
The painting's compositional balance is created by the series of parallel verticals that are made by the masts. By making both the central mast and its reflection almost touch the physical edge of the canvas, Monet has created a play between the imaginary space and the painting's actual surface.

PINK CHATEAU
This elegant château can be seen in the centre of the horizon, depicted with only a few strokes of paint.

COLOUR CONTRASTS
Monet has used complementary colours – red and green, blue and orange, yellow and violet. Yellow highlights, for example, contrast with violet shadows. When these colours are placed side-by-side, each heightens the visual effect of its opposite.

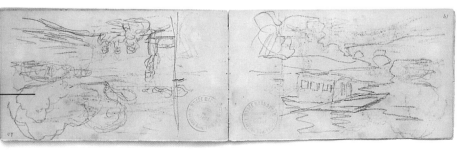

Drawn the other way up is a sketch of figures on a riverbank

THE FLOATING STUDIO
Monet included his floating studio as a motif in several of his paintings, and one of them shows a similar view to this little sketch. In both sketch and painting, the studio is moored in isolation on the River Seine, with reflections snaking below it, against a background of a wooded riverbank. Since the studio is empty, the canopy is not extended.

The Impressionist shows

Nadar's studios

A MOCKING RESPONSE
Something of the tone of Leroy's article can be gathered from the mock horror of this caricature.

MONET AND HIS ASSOCIATES, spurred on partly by their rejection of the Salon, and partly by the Salon jury's repeated rejection of them, decided to put together an independent exhibition of their own. The photographer, Félix Tournachon – known as Nadar – lent the group of artists the spacious second-floor studios that he had vacated on the fashionable Boulevard des Capucines.

On 15 April 1874, 30 members of the newly formed "Société Anonyme des Artistes Peintres, Sculpteurs, Graveurs, etc." put on their first joint show. Among the artists were Monet, Auguste Renoir, Alfred Sisley, Camille Pissarro, Edgar Degas, Paul Cézanne, Berthe Morisot, and Eugène Boudin. The first four, in particular, showed marked similarities in their work, but the "Société Anonyme" itself had no group style or identity; exhibitors were drawn together by a common opposition to "tame" official art. The group identity was really created ten days after the show opened, when a satirical reviewer, Louis Leroy, attached a label to them – one that would stick forever. Taking as his starting point one of the 12 exhibits submitted by Monet – *Impression, Sunrise* (below) – Leroy sarcastically entitled his article "Exhibition of the Impressionists".

THE FIRST EXHIBITION *above*
Monet exhibited five oils and seven pastels in the 1874 exhibition. As part of the spirit of cooperation, exhibitors agreed to donate one-tenth of their sales to cover the expenses.

Impression, Sunrise

1872; 48 x 63 cm (19 x 24¾ in)
For the title of this view of Le Havre, Monet chose a term that had been used to describe freely handled landscapes by artists such as Daubigny and Jongkind, among others. Leroy seized on the title to focus his attack on the show, saying, *"Impression ...* Wallpaper in its embryonic state is more finished than that seascape". Ironically, with its thin, muted washes, rather than broken patches of pure colour, this picture is not typical of Monet's "Impressionist style".

WOMAN IN THE GREEN DRESS
1866; 2 m 31 cm x 1 m 51 cm
(7 ft 6 in x 4 ft 9½ in)
Although the Salon gave highest status to history painting and conservative, formal portraiture, it did allow for some innovation: Jongkind and Courbet had been medal winners, and the Salon jury included both Corot and Daubigny. Monet had two seascapes accepted (and praised) in 1865, and this life-size painting of Camille was one of the Salon triumphs in 1866.

VIEWS OF THE SALON *left and above*
At the Salon, paintings were stacked almost from floor to ceiling. Less conventional paintings were often hung at the top, where they could barely be seen from ground level. By 1879, when the illustration above was produced, the monopoly of the Salon was under threat: the 1863 Salon des Refusés had exhibited the 4,000 paintings rejected by the Salon jury; and in 1867, Edouard Manet and Gustave Courbet had shown in their own pavilions at the World's Fair, which gave Monet and his friends the idea for an independent group exhibition.

PAUL DURAND-RUEL *right*
As the Salon's grip on the French art world loosened, specialist picture dealers came into being. Paul Durand-Ruel, the first and the most important commercial champion of the Impressionists, sold his art materials shop in 1869 in order to concentrate on dealing. He bought premises between rue le Peletier and rue Laffitte, where several of the Impressionist exhibitions, and later one-man shows, were held.

CLAUDE MONET
Auguste Renoir; 1875; 85 x 60.5 cm (33½ x 23¾ in)
Renoir painted this portrait in the year that Durand-Ruel organized a public auction of Impressionist works at the Hotel Drouot. The dealer recalled: "The insults that were thrown at us – especially at Monet and Renoir! The public howled and treated us as imbeciles.... Works sold for as little as 50 francs – and that was only because of the frames".

THE GROUP BREAKS UP
Monet did not exhibit in all eight Impressionist exhibitions. He showed in the first four, but not in the fifth, in 1880. That year, anxious to gain money and recognition, he had a solo show at the offices of *La Vie Moderne* magazine; and the Salon accepted a picture. Personal and stylistic rifts were breaking up the group. Like Renoir and Sisley, Monet refused to take part in the final exhibition of 1886 (above).

Images of steam

Trains, frequently shown steaming across the railway bridge at Argenteuil, had featured in Monet's work for some years before January 1877, when he began a number of paintings of Gare Saint-Lazare. Still based in Argenteuil (p. 20), he rented a small apartment in Paris near the station, and during the next few months he painted 12 different views of it. It seems the railway authorities not only allowed him to paint there, but also agreed to hold back trains while he worked.

EASY JOURNEY
Monet lived a minute's walk away from Argenteuil station (right), where trains ran often to Saint-Lazare.

Argenteuil to Paris train timetable

DEPARTURE TIME *left*
One of several sketches Monet made of Saint-Lazare, this shows a train leaving the station. It is closely related to another painting in the series.

The diagonal of the platform leads the eye into the picture

Decisive framing lines

Gare Saint-Lazare

1877; 54 x 73.5 cm (21¼ x 29 in)
For some of his paintings of Saint-Lazare, Monet set up his easel outside among the sidings. This is one of four canvases that he painted inside the terminus. Its aggressively modern, urban theme was startling at the time and remains so, though Monet's fascination with Saint-Lazare probably had less to do with the station's modernity than with the dramatic atmospheric effects created by the steam billowing from the locomotives.

TRAIN IN THE SNOW
1875; 59 x 78 cm (23 x 30¾ in)
Two years before his Saint-Lazare pictures, Monet painted this locomotive at the station at Argenteuil. The red front and yellow lights of the engine stand out against the train's iron blackness, which is muffled by misty, mid-winter air. Coloured shadows are cast in the snow.

METAL AND STEAM

The inverted V of the pitched roof dominates the composition. The dark lines of the roof provide a powerful contrast to the fluffy, blue-grey clouds of steam and the luminous grey sky. Monet has only thinly covered the sky area (see back-lit photograph below), allowing the pale ground to glow through. He has deliberately left a "reserve" in the dark roof area on the right, which he has then covered with sketchily applied flicks of grey.

COLOUR OF BLACK

The canopy, engines, and figures appear black, but actually contain little black pigment. Monet has created the effect by combining various bright colours – blues, greens, and reds.

FINISHING TOUCHES

Monet enlivened the surface with vivid dabs and streaks of vermilion, blue, and green – added when the previously applied paint was not quite dry. The red-brown signature, now indistinct, was also added at this final stage. In the corners of the canvas are holes in which Monet inserted pins with which to carry home the wet canvas.

SUPPLIERS' STAMPS
Still visible on the back of the picture are the stamps of the canvas supplier, Deforgue Carpentier (above), and the stretcher maker, E. Hostellet (below). This is a pre-stretched, pre-primed canvas.

Puffs of grey smoke partly obscure the dark roof

Main shapes were blocked in with dark washes at the start

THICK AND THIN
This photograph, taken while the painting was strongly lit from behind, vividly reveals the different thicknesses of paint. Orange light shines through the thinnest layers, such as the area on the top right, where Monet did not paint in the roof but left the primed canvas to be sketchily covered by a cloud of steam. The areas that remain darkest are the most thickly painted – the trains, the figures in the foreground, and the wall and roof of the station.

Monet's two families

Camille Monet

MONET FIRST MET Alice and Ernest Hoschedé in the summer of 1876, when he was invited to stay and work at their luxurious château outside Paris. A year later, the lavish lifestyle of the Hoschedés came to a brutal end when Ernest was declared bankrupt. Unable to face the situation, he abandoned the pregnant Alice and their five children. By this time, the Monet and Hoschedé families had become close friends and after the château was seized, Alice and her children joined Monet, Camille, and Jean to share a house in the village of Vétheuil. The two families would be entwined forever.

Studio portrait of Alice Hoschedé

(Left to right) Suzanne, Blanche, Germaine, and Marthe Hoschedé

THE TURKEYS
1877; 172 x 175 cm (68½ x 68 in)
This is one of four large-scale "decorations" that Hoschedé commissioned Monet to paint for his château (depicted here) at Montergon, near Paris.

Fall from grace

Alice's sophisticated, enlightened, but respectable way of life was replaced by one of initial poverty and continued unorthodoxy. Though her marriage to Ernest was over, and she and Monet lived as man and wife after Camille's death in 1879, her religion prohibited divorce. Only after Ernest's death in 1891 could she become "Madame Monet".

Ernest Hoschedé: patron of the arts, and bankrupt

INTIMATE SCENE *right*
For some time, the cramped Monet-Hoschedé household comprised three adults and eight children. But this later sketch of the children intently at work around a table suggests a contented home.

VÉTHEUIL, SEEN FROM LAVACOURT
1879; 60 x 81 cm (23½ x 32 in)
Argenteuil – Monet's home during the 1870s, and the focus of the period of "pure Impressionism" – had grown increasingly industrialized. In 1878, Monet left there for the unspoilt village of Vétheuil, "a ravishing spot on the banks of the Seine", further out from Paris. This painting reveals the rural, riverside delights that enchanted him. "I've become a country-dweller once again," he wrote to one of his friends, "I only come to Paris rarely, to sell my canvases". The move into the countryside marked a change in his work. The days when he enjoyed painting alongside his friends were over; and views of people at leisure in a suburban landscape were mostly replaced by timeless images of nature in the raw.

A portrait of Papa?

THE YOUNGEST CHILDREN
Monet probably made this pastel study of Michel Monet and Jean-Pierre Hoschedé in 1881. That year, for the sake of the older children's schooling, the joint family moved from Vétheuil to Poissy. At around that time, Monet began his painting trips away from home, leaving Alice to care for the children.

MICHEL MONET
This unusually detailed drawing shows Michel, Monet's youngest and sole surviving son, who eventually inherited the Giverny estate (pp. 34–35). After his death in 1966, the house and contents were left to the French nation. The magnificent Monet collection at the Musée Marmottan in Paris is from the Michel Monet legacy.

MARRIAGE TIES
Family relationships became even more entwined over the years: Blanche married Jean Monet; Suzanne wed the painter, Theodore Butler. After her death, he married Marthe. Monet made Germaine (above) break off with Alfred Sisley's son.

Camille's final portrait

MONET'S FIRST WIFE, CAMILLE, had been frail and ill since before the birth of their second son, Michel, in March 1878. When Camille finally died in September 1879 at the age of 32, Monet lost not only a wife but also his favourite model. Years later he remembered how he had been appalled to find himself studying her dead face with more of the dispassionate scrutiny of an artist than the sadness of a bereaved husband: "I found myself staring at those tragic features, and automatically trying to identify the sequence, the gradations of colour that death had imposed on the motionless face … even before the thought occurred to me to memorize the face that had meant so much to me, my first involuntary response was to tremble at the shock of the colours".

**PORTRAIT OF
MICHEL IN A POMPOM HAT**
1880; 46 x 38 cm (18 x 15 in)
Monet made this portrait of his infant son the year after Camille died. The artist was living in Vétheuil at the time, with Alice and the eight Monet and Hoschedé children (p. 28).

Camille on her Deathbed
1879; 90 x 68 cm (35½ x 26¾ in)
As in many of his pictures of Camille, her face is obscured by a veil; but here the veil is her shroud. Startling details, such as the way her lips have pulled back in death, imbue the portrait with a chilling sense of immediacy.

THE ARTIST'S FAMILY
A rare document, this census was taken in 1876 at Argenteuil, when Monet was 36 years old, Camille 29, and Jean 9.

2243	26	Monet	Claude	Artiste Peintre		1		36
	27	Onorine fme Monet	Camille	"			1	29
	28	Monet	Jean	"		1		9

RED FLOWERS
Camille's wraith-like face and body seem to disintegrate into the loosely painted, pale grey shroud made of gauze. A bouquet of flowers on her chest adds a subtle glimpse of colour.

THE PROMENADE
1875; 100 x 81 cm (39¼ x 32 in)
Painted four years before Camille's death, this is one of Monet's most delightful pictures of her. It shows her walking with Jean on top of a hill. A summer breeze carries the wisps of her veil across her face as she turns to look down towards the artist. Lit from behind, she appears surrounded by a halo of sunlight.

STAMPED-ON SIGNATURE
Monet's black signature stands out starkly against the partially covered canvas. He did not sign the painting himself – it was stamped with his signature after his death.

Dress and sky are similar in colour, but back-lighting ensures that the figure stands out

VETHEUIL IN THE FOG
1879; 60 x 71 cm (23½ x 28 in)
A severe winter followed Camille's death. The subdued tones of this painting probably reflect the atmospheric conditions at that time, rather than Monet's state of mind.

Figures in landscapes

In the mid-1880s, Monet decided to tackle an ambitious group of paintings of figures in landscapes. The work shown below is probably one of the first, and is paired with another that has the figure turned to the right. Both compositions are reworkings of *The Promenade* (p. 30), depicting Camille and Jean on a hill, but they can also be seen as a challenge to Georges Seurat's gigantic figure painting, *La Grande Jatte*. Here the model is Suzanne – Alice Hoschedé's daughter (p. 28), and Monet's favourite model after the death of Camille. He had planned to employ a professional model at Giverny for these paintings of figures in landscapes, but Alice told him bluntly that if a model set foot in the house, she would leave it.

The Promenade (p. 30); (p. 28)

Lead white   Cobalt violet   Cobalt blue

Viridian   Emerald green   Cadmium yellow

Vermilion   Red lake

ARTIST'S PALETTE
The pigments Monet used probably include those above. For the top three-quarters of the painting, he has mixed his colours with large amounts of lead white to create a delicate essay in pastel blues, pale pinks, and a soft absinthe green. By contrast, the grass is in darker, more varied colours. But the subtly multi-coloured whites of the dress reflect the pigments from both areas, unifying the picture's surface.

Woman with a Parasol

1886; 131 x 88 cm (51½ x 34½ in)
Subtitled *Turned to the Left*, this painting was executed 11 years after *The Promenade*. Monet has placed the figure high above him on top of a hill, with her back to a breeze. The curve of her body continues through the broad sweep of shadow.

ON THE HORIZON

Monet has roughly scrubbed the sky and clouds in varying directions and then allowed the paint of the clouds to dry before adding long, impasted streaks of pinkish grass on the horizon. Though pale, these streaks stand out well against the cloud and form a tonal bridge between the white of the cloud and the darkness of the shadow that lies further down the canvas.

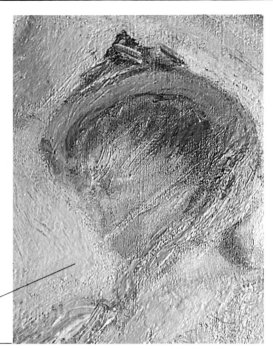

Heavily worked area of absinthe green fills in the space between the face and the blue ribbon

Impasted streaks of paint cast real shadows on the picture surface

Dark green (viridian) of grass against pale pink dress

BEHIND THE PAINTED VEIL

Monet has depersonalized his figure, obliterating all her facial features with the veil that is swept across her face. Framed by the luminous green of her parasol, she does not turn to look at the artist, as Camille does in *The Promenade*, but instead appears to gaze impassively into the distance.

Flicks of bright yellow create sun-drenched highlights

DRESS AND SKY

Suffused with pink and blue, the white dress is more heavily worked than the rest of the picture, with stiffish paint. A vigorous, streak of blue shadow effectively links the fabric with the sky.

VIRTUOSO BRUSHWORK

The treatment of the grass is an astonishingly dynamic display: comma-like flicks of colour evoke individual stalks of windswept grass; and sunlit strokes of pink and yellow contrast with the dark greens, reds, and purples of the shadow. The tangle of brushstrokes sets up a rhythm that is continued in the sky and seems to encircle the figure.

Established at Giverny

THE PLAINS OF GIVERNY
Giverny nestles beneath Normandy hills. To the south-west, fields and meadows stretch to the River Seine.

"I AM FILLED WITH DELIGHT. Giverny is a splendid place for me." Leaving behind the hated Poissy (p. 29), Monet discovered the quiet village of Giverny, some 50 miles outside Paris. He, Alice, and the children (pp. 28–29) arrived in 1883, and it was to remain the family home for good. But the pleasure of moving in was marred by the sad news that Edouard Manet had died. Monet left for the capital to be a pall-bearer to the unofficial leader of "modern art". That year also saw the first of Monet's solo shows at Durand-Ruel's. It was greeted with indifference, though soon the artist's fortunes were to change, largely thanks to an exhibition that Durand-Ruel held in New York in 1886. American enthusiasm was to encourage French appreciation and, after a huge retrospective show three years later, Monet's reputation was sealed.

A LASTING HOME
Monet and the family stayed at an inn before settling into the pink, shuttered house known as *La Pressoir* – the Cider Press (above). After Michel Monet's death in 1966, the house was bestowed to the Académie des Beaux-Arts. Now restored, it is open to the public.

LA GRANDE ALLEE
Monet immediately began transforming the garden (p. 52). Changes to *La Grande Allée* (right) provoked family rows: in the end, funereal spruce and cypress were replaced by roses and nasturtiums.

AN UNUSUAL FAMILY
The family poses in the garden, some years after arriving at Giverny. Clockwise from the bottom left are: Michel Monet, Alice Hoschedé, Claude Monet, Jean-Pierre Hoschedé, Blanche Hoschedé, Jean Monet, Jacques Hoschedé, Marthe Hoschedé (at the front), Germaine Hoschedé, and Suzanne Hoschedé. They remained outsiders in the farming community, where Monet's "bohemian" career and the unconventional nature of his household were viewed with considerable suspicion.

DINING AT GIVERNY
Mealtimes in the yellow dining-room were the focus of family life at Giverny. Monet and Alice had gourmet tastes, which they indulged whether they could afford to or not. Monet's working day began at dawn and ended with dinner at seven o'clock.

FINANCIAL BACKING

Between 1873 and 1880, Durand-Ruel had been unable to buy Monet's paintings. But when the dealer's financial situation improved, so did Monet's. During the early years at Giverny, he earned about 30,000 francs a year from "Monsieur Durand", who made regular payments to him (below), organized payment for his painting materials (right), and even settled his tailor's bill.

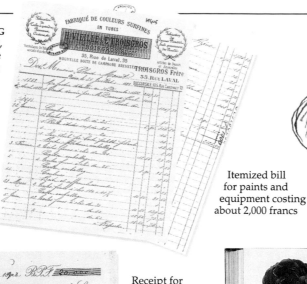

Itemized bill for paints and equipment costing about 2,000 francs

Receipt for 20,000 francs, paid by Durand-Ruel to Monet

Monet annotated his drawing "pale mauve"

SINGLE BLOOM

Irises were among Monet's favourite flowers, and he planted them throughout the garden. This drawing is a late addition to one of his sketchbooks.

WHITE CLEMATIS

1887; 92 x 52 cm; (36¼ x 20½ in)
Monet was anxious to establish the flower garden quickly, both to have motifs to paint indoors on rainy days, and to paint in the garden when the sun shone. This flower-filled canvas may depict a clematis that grew in the garden.

MONET'S BOOKS

Monet loved books – perhaps his greatest treasure was the *Journal* by the Romantic master and supreme colourist, Eugène Delacroix. He had an extensive botanical library at Giverny that included a 26-volume set of *Flowers of the Gardens of Europe* (above).

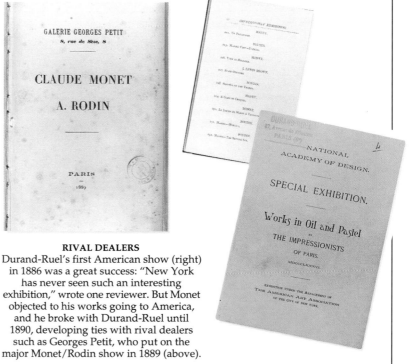

RIVAL DEALERS

Durand-Ruel's first American show (right) in 1886 was a great success: "New York has never seen such an interesting exhibition," wrote one reviewer. But Monet objected to his works going to America, and he broke with Durand-Ruel until 1890, developing ties with rival dealers such as Georges Petit, who put on the major Monet/Rodin show in 1889 (above).

Boat among the grasses

CONTENTEDLY ESTABLISHED at Giverny (p. 34), Monet painted several dreamily poetic canvases of Alice's daughters – Blanche and Suzanne – in boats on the River Epte, which ran near the house. He probably intended the composition opposite to be one of them, since in the preliminary sketch (right) there is an indication of a figure in the prow, but the girls fell ill and would have been unable to pose. This work may be the one to which the artist refers in a letter to his friend, Gustave Geffroy, on 22 June 1890: "I have once again taken up things that are impossible to do – water with grasses that undulate below the surface".
These words are typical of Monet, who often set himself difficult tasks such as this, to stretch himself and to prove his ability and versatility.

HORIZONTAL SKETCH
Monet's sketchbooks contain three sketches related to *The Boat*: two with a horizontal format and one vertical, like the painting. In this horizontal version, there is a subtle but significant difference in the positioning of the boat. Here it touches the top edge of the page and is not cropped at the right.

GIRLS IN WHITE DRESSES
This is one of numerous sketches related to pictures of the Hoschedé girls in boats. Their fashionable dresses and relaxed poses echo paintings by Monet's English colleague, John Singer Sargent. Monet's pictures have also been linked to a prose-poem by Stéphane Mallarmé – *The White Water Lily* (1885). This sketch was probably drawn in 1887. It was in the summer of 1890, when Monet was working on *The Boat*, that the girls fell ill.

Dress with leg-of-mutton sleeves and narrow waist in vogue at that time

Front of boat cropped off by edge of page

MONET'S BOAT AT GIVERNY
A replica of Monet's *norvégienne* – the broad, square-ended rowing boat that appears in *The Boat* – has been built at Giverny. It is still used to clear the underwater weed that grows in the waterlily pond there.

The Boat

c.1887–90;
146 x 133 cm (57½ x 52¼ in)
This painting, with its strikingly asymmetrical and empty composition, depicts one of Monet's boats moored under the trees on the River Epte. The picture has much in common with Japanese art. By using an extreme, high viewpoint, Monet has effectively flattened the image and removed any naturalistic sense of space or point of focus.
The undulating weeds beneath the water seem to hang in waving ribbons.

CUT-OUTS
Monet has established the spatial relationships between the pictorial elements with overlapping layers. This was a technique used in Japanese prints, such as those in Monet's collection at Giverny. The broad leaves appear to have been cut out and stuck on to the surface, over the simple shape of the boat, helping to flatten the pictorial space and emphasize the decorative qualities of the work.

FROM ABOVE
The rowing boat forms a pale, elliptical shape that touches the edge of the canvas and seems held in place by the angles of the top right-hand corner of the picture. The boat is painted very loosely, perhaps in anticipation of a seated figure being added in the prow.

"THINGS IMPOSSIBLE"
The most astonishing aspect of the work is the fact that more than three-quarters of the huge canvas is covered by the threads of thin underwater grasses. These are based upon Monet's observation of the long weeds that were caught by the current. But he did not depict them receding into the distance as they would have appeared in nature; the sinuous ribbons of green, red, yellow, and blue flow down and across the surface of the painting in an abstract pattern.

Painting campaigns

WITH DURAND-RUEL PROVIDING AN INCOME, and Alice to look after the children, Monet embarked upon a series of painting campaigns, which took him away from home for prolonged periods during the 1880s. The Normandy coast was the focus of his attention and he made repeated trips to certain favoured sites, such as Pourville, Fécamp, Dieppe, Varengeville, and Etretat. He was especially drawn to the spectacular aspects of nature during this period: the vertiginous cliffs that dropped abruptly into the Channel; the côte sauvage (wild coast) of Belle-Ile in Brittany, where Atlantic rollers crashed against granite rocks; the dramatic Creuse valley in central France; and the sun-drenched landscapes of the Côte d'Azur. Throughout these campaigns, he wrote frequently to his friends, and daily to Alice, obsessively describing his work: the search for motifs, the struggles with the weather, the challenges posed by the light, his elation when the work went well, and his despair when it did not.

A BASE IN NORMANDY
Monet lived and worked mainly in the north-west region of France.

Pourville · Dieppe
Fécamp
Etretat
Le Havre
Rouen
Trouville
Giverny
Vétheuil
Argenteuil
PARIS

THE VALLEY OF THE SEINE
Monet loved to live and work beside water. His favourite homes – Argenteuil, Vétheuil, and Giverny – lie along the meandering route of the Seine between Paris and Le Havre. During the 1880s, he frequently made painting trips along the familiar Channel coastline of his youth.

*Pourville,
15 February 1882*

DAILY CORRESPONDENCE *left*
The consecutive dates of these letters from Pourville indicate the frequency of Monet's correspondence. Alice wrote back daily – occasional gaps triggered anxious letters from the artist. Yet it was some years before he dropped the formal "Chère Madame" for "Ma chère Alice".

*Pourville,
14 February
1882*

Loving letters

Monet was not the easiest man to get along with – he was egotistical, obsessed with his work, moody, competitive, and, when it came to business matters, driven by self-interest. But the hundreds of letters he wrote to Alice reveal the tender side of his nature. From Bordighera, in the south of France, for example, he wrote: "When I have finished my day's work, and I am alone in my sad hotel room, I don't stop thinking about you ... I am lucky to be working in this beautiful country, but my heart is always, always at Giverny".

Monet's
letter opener

Monet's
quill pen

WAITING AT HOME *right*
It was only a few years since Alice's husband, Ernest, had left, and the long separations from Monet were difficult for her to bear. From Etretat in 1883, he reassured her: "Have courage, this absence won't last long ... I love you".

THE CLIFF AT FECAMP
1881; 64 x 80 cm (25 x 31½ in)
In 1881 and 1882, Monet spent months painting the cliffs around Dieppe. This bold, asymmetrical composition is typical of the many works he made, with clifftop to one side, and sea and sky to the other. Rather than employing linear perspective to lead the eye into the distance, Monet has created an abrupt transition from the foreground to the background. He has also divided the canvas into a simple pattern of three parts.

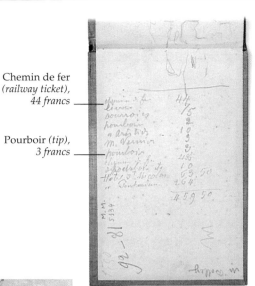

Chemin de fer (railway ticket), 44 francs

Pourboir (tip), 3 francs

ACCOUNTING DETAILS *above*
Monet could be both extravagant and mean with money. This list of his expenditure during a trip, which he jotted down in the back of a sketchbook, demonstrates his penny-pinching side: he has even recorded a tip of three francs.

ANTIBES
1888; 65 x 92 cm (25½ x 36¼ in)
Monet travelled to the Côte d'Azur with Auguste Renoir in December 1883 and returned there the next month to work alone. At Bordighera, he had trouble finding motifs: "It is too thickly wooded," he wrote to Alice, continuing, "... I am really a man for isolated trees and wide-open spaces". Though he discovered such motifs at nearby Antibes, the brilliant light of the Mediterranean caused problems; Monet felt that he needed to heighten his palette to one of "diamonds and precious stones" so that he could render such intense colours. In 1888, he returned South to paint landscapes such as this one in "white, pink, and blue, all enveloped in this magical air".

WILD COAST, BELLE-ILE
1886; 65 x 81 cm (25½ x 32 in)
Monet produced 39 pictures at Belle-Ile in 1886, including this one. He had not painted the Atlantic coast before: "The Ocean is something completely different," he said. "You know my passion for the sea," he wrote to Alice. Though bad weather hampered his stay, he painted "in the wind and the rain", and echoed the dramatic violence of the waves against the dark rocks with a harsher palette and with expressively vigorous brushwork.

FOREIGN TRAVEL
Apart from a trip to Holland in 1886 to paint the tulip fields, Monet rarely painted abroad unless he could combine work with a visit to relatives. In 1895, he visited Scandinavia, where his step-son, Jacques, lived. He stayed in an artists' colony in Sandviken, painting outside in conditions so cold that there were icicles in his beard. This drawing is from his Norwegian sketchbook.

The series paintings

AUTUMN LANDSCAPE
At the end of summer, the fields near
Monet's house at Giverny would be
dotted with conical grainstacks. He had
painted them since 1884, but only
began treating them as a series in 1890.

Throughout his career, Monet had painted repeated views of the same subject. But from 1890, he began working on coherent series of paintings: *Grainstacks, Poplars, Rouen Cathedral* (pp. 44–47), and *Mornings*. This new development reflected Monet's increasing preoccupation with what he called "instantaneity", the atmospheric envelope of light that unifies a scene for a moment, before changing to create a new overall effect. As the effect altered, so Monet changed to another canvas. Intending these works to be viewed together, he began them outdoors, but "harmonized" them in the studio.

PRELIMINARY NOTES
Monet made several sketches in which
he shifted viewpoints to change the
relative positions of the stacks.

The Grainstacks series

Monet's first series show was held at Durand-Ruel's in May 1891. Featuring 15 *Grainstacks* and several other works, including *Woman with a Parasol* (p. 32), it had been eagerly anticipated for some months, and was a critical and commercial triumph. Monet's repeated images of the simplified forms of the stacks, enveloped and irradiated with coloured light, captured the imagination of critics, collectors, and artists alike.

GRAINSTACKS, SNOW EFFECT
1890–91; 65 x 92 cm (25½ x 36¼ in)
In this powerfully simple
picture, two stacks stand alone
in a snow-covered landscape,
wrapped in an almost tangibly
snow-filled atmosphere. Lit
from behind, all their detail is
lost and they are reduced to
geometric shapes that cast pale
blue lozenges of shadow on
the pinkish snow.

**GRAINSTACKS,
END OF SUMMER**
1890–91; 60 x 100 cm (23½ x 39¼ in)
Here the stacks are bathed in
the shimmering, golden light
of late summer. Monet thought
that the paintings only gained
their full value by comparison
with the others. It was not so
much the grainstacks that
interested him, but the way
they changed with the light:
"For me, a landscape ... exists
by virtue of the air and light
that surround it," he said.

The Poplars series

A group of tall poplar trees that lined the banks of the River Epte, 1¼ miles (2 km) from Giverny, became the subject of Monet's second series. He had begun work in the summer of 1891, when the project was threatened with being literally cut short: since the trees had grown to their required height, they were being auctioned off for timber. Monet struck a deal with a local timber merchant, paying him to postpone cutting down the poplars until he had finished painting them.

JAPANESE SERIES
Pictorial series were a feature of the Japanese art Monet so admired. This tree-lined landscape by Ando Hiroshige is one of *69 Stations on the Kisokaido* (c.1835–42).

A RARE VIEW
Over the years, Monet's series paintings were sold separately and dispersed worldwide. In 1989–90, they were exhibited together in Boston, Chicago, and London.

POPLARS ON THE BANKS OF THE EPTE
1891; 81.5 x 82 cm (32 x 32¼ in)
In this painting, Monet has chosen a more oblique and distant viewpoint from that of the left-hand picture. This combines with the angle of the reflections to create a symmetrical, triangle-based image. The delicate colours and the tremulous effect of sunlight on water and leaves add to the decorative beauty of the image.

POPLARS ON THE BANKS OF THE EPTE
1891; 92 x 73 cm (36¼ x 28¾ in)
The poplars towered over Monet as he worked from his floating studio. This picture is unusually freely handled, but as in the two *Grainstacks* (opposite), there is rigorous simplicity in the composition. The trunks form a linear grid that covers most of the canvas.

MORNING ON THE SEINE
1896–97; 73 x 92 cm (28¾ x 36¾ in)
In 1896, when he was 56 years old, Monet began a series of dawn paintings of a branch of the Seine near Giverny. He would rise at 3.30 am and walk across dew-covered fields to set to work before the riverbank had emerged from the mist. Many compared these poetic views to the landscapes of Camille Corot (p. 10).

SERIES EXHIBITIONS
Monet exhibited 15 *Poplars* at Durand-Ruel's in 1892 – the first show limited to a single series. It was a great success. In 1898, Georges Petit put on a major Monet show. As pre-publicity, an entire supplement in *Le Gaulois* paper was devoted to the artist.

Cathedral series

MONET SAID that the idea for this series originated when he observed the effects of sunlight on a country church, as the "sun's rays slowly dissolved the mists ... that wrapped the golden stone in an ideally vaporous envelope". In 1892, he set up a studio above a draper's shop opposite Rouen Cathedral, and worked from February to April on up to 14 canvases in a day. The following year, he returned to continue, this time from an apartment a few doors away. He struggled on, determined but often despondent. "It's a stubborn crust of colour," he wrote to Alice, "but it's not a painting". When he eventually exhibited 20 of the *Cathedrals* at Durand-Ruel's in May 1895, they sold for an astonishing 15,000 francs each.

ROUEN PHOTOGRAPH
Monet owned several photographs of Rouen Cathedral, including this one.

Harmony in Blue and Gold

1894; 107 x 73 cm (42 x 28¾ in)
This painting's full title is *Rouen Cathedral, Full Sunlight – Harmony in Blue and Gold*. Monet selected a very close vantage point for these paintings and, most commonly, this slanted, south-west view. The sun would rise behind the Tour d'Albane and cast afternoon shadows across the carved west front, accentuating the cavernous hollows of the portals and the large rose window.

GOTHIC TOWER
The top and sides of the Tour d'Albane (on the left of the picture) are cropped off by the edge of the canvas; the sun-bleached pinnacles of the nave roof stand out against a blue sky.

COLOURFUL LINES
Monet wanted to "do architecture without lines". Using colour rather than contour, he has managed to describe both the surface detail of the Gothic façade and the massive building's sense of solid structure.

SKETCHES OF ROUEN
(Above) Among Monet's many sketches of Rouen, this forcefully drawn one shows the cathedral towering over houses. (Below) With its trembling delicacy, this somehow parallels the shimmering effect of the paintings.

A CHANGE
OF ANGLE
This is the only
finished version
of a frontal view
of the west façade.
Analysis has shown
that it was begun
as a south-west
view like most of
the others; Monet
may have altered
the angle to add
variety to the series.

GREY DAYS
The cathedral
façade seen (as here)
in the diffuse, soft
light of an overcast
day, appeared in one
group of canvases in
the series. Monet's
close friend, Georges
Clemenceau, devoted
the front page of his
newspaper (*La Justice*)
to a laudatory article
on the series and also
identified four sub-
groups: grey, white,
rainbow, and blue.

**ROUEN CATHEDRAL, THE PORTAL SEEN
FROM THE FRONT – HARMONY IN BROWN**
1894; 107 x 73 cm (42 x 28¾ in)

**ROUEN CATHEDRAL,
THE PORTAL, GREY WEATHER**
1894; 100 x 65 cm (39¼ x 25½ in)

WHITE MIST
White, blue,
and burnt orange
combine in this
version. Compared
with *Harmony in Blue
and Gold* (opposite
page), the stone of the
façade has been
further softened by
a misty morning's
atmospheric *enveloppe*.
Against a pale sky,
the pinnacles of the
nave roof become
blue silhouettes.

SENSE OF SCALE
A slight shift
in viewpoint, and the
little houses huddling
at the foot of the Tour
d'Albane are included
in the picture, helping
to emphasize the vast
proportions of the
cathedral. The flock of
birds around the tower
also contribute to the
sense of scale. In other
canvases, Monet added
human figures.

**ROUEN CATHEDRAL,
MORNING SUN, HARMONY IN BLUE**
1894; 91 x 63 cm (35¾ x 24¾ in)

**ROUEN CATHEDRAL, THE PORTAL
AND THE TOWER OF SAINT-ROMAIN,
MORNING EFFECT, HARMONY IN WHITE**
1892–94; 106 x 75 cm (41¾ x 29½ in)

Study of light on stone

A STONE FAÇADE might seem an unusual choice of motif for an artist as dedicated to painting nature as Monet, but light changes even stone, as the *Cathedral* series shows (pp. 44–45). In the finished canvases, Monet built up the layers of paint so heavily that some critics compared the texture of the paintings to the carved stone surface itself. Yet the thick encrustations of paint seem to dissolve as well as depict the façade. This unfinished painting (right), abandoned before Monet had built up the unified web of colour that covers the surface of his completed canvases, gives a rare insight into the process by which he achieved his effect.

End of the Day

1892–3; 100 x 65 cm (39¼ x 25½ in)
The full title of this painting is *Rouen Cathedral, Sun Effect, End of the Day*. The result of just a few sessions of work, it is a powerfully vibrant picture that remained incomplete and unsigned at Monet's death. His signature has been stamped on later in black.

Lead white

Cobalt violet

Cobalt blue

Ultramarine

Vermilion

Cadmium orange

Cadmium yellow

ARTIST'S PALETTE *above*
Many of the *Cathedral* canvases are characterized by their dominant colour themes. Here, as in other versions (pp. 44–45), blue and gold predominate, and the pigments shown above are probably among those that Monet used. The upper part of the façade glows in the sunset, while cool, blue shadows flood across, and into, the portals.

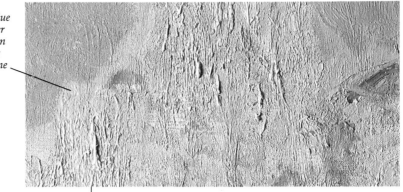

A paler blue underlayer can be seen where sky meets stone

SKY AND STONE

Although Monet has selected an extremely close-up view, the patch of sky sets the façade in context and provides a contrast in colour and texture. Blue is a "cool" colour and appears to recede. Against this blue, the "warmer" pinks and golden yellows of the building appear to come forward, and stand out. Monet also made a feature of the decorative pattern created where the triangle of Gothic pinnacles pierces the sky.

Ridges of paint echo the curved lines of the carved stone

SURFACE TEXTURE

This photograph has been taken in raking (angled) light to accentuate the raised texture of the paint. In the finished paintings (pp. 44–45), brushstrokes become woven into a continuous, chalky web of paint, but individual strokes are still distinct here. Their direction echoes the lines of the pointed arch.

Lines of mauve depict the window's carved hood

In sunlight and shadow, orange mingles with mauve

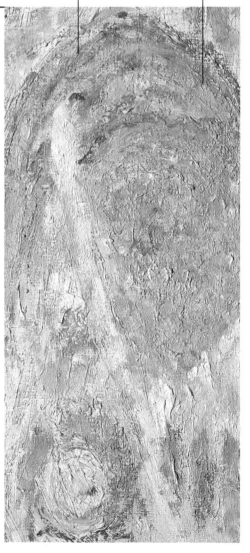

White impasted highlight

IN THE SHADOWS *left*

The subtly unified surface has not yet been built up. At this early stage of the painting, a blue shadow slashes across the façade; trails of dark blue, orange, and violet suggest the curve of the left portal; and an *impasto* highlight in white indicates the carved buttress.

LINES AND DOTS *right*

The architectural geometry of the façade imbues the painting with a strong sense of structure: the elongated triangle that is above the doorway projects in front of the circle of the rose window. Dots of mauve, pink, and orange paint recreate the mottled effect of stained glass.

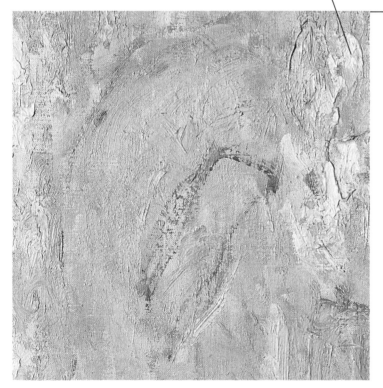

Travels in later life

Savoy Hotel in 1899

AFTER HIS MARRIAGE TO ALICE IN 1892, Monet made few of the long painting campaigns that had occupied so much of the previous decade (pp. 38–39). He did have a plan to paint all his old motifs once more, but after trips to the Normandy coast and to Vétheuil, the project fizzled out. In February 1899, great sadness struck when his step-daughter, Suzanne, died, after suffering from a lingering illness. Alice was completely broken for a time, and Monet hardly dared leave her. He took her to London in the autumn of that year, staying at the new Savoy Hotel that overlooked the River Thames. He later returned there alone to work during the next two winters. At around this time, he and Alice acquired a new toy – an automobile. They would often set off on chauffeur-driven trips, even driving down to Spain in 1904 to see the Velázquez paintings in the Prado. Visits to Venice in 1908 and 1909 marked the end of Monet's travels. From then on, Giverny was his world.

LONDON NEWS
Monet wrote this letter to Germaine on a "melancholy Sunday" in March 1900.

PASTEL VIEW OF WATERLOO BRIDGE
Monet probably made this pastel in January 1901, as he waited at the Savoy for his canvases to arrive from France. He had not used pastels for years, but he found them well-suited to rendering the misty atmosphere. He told Alice that it was pastels that had suggested a way forward for his painting.

Pastel sticks

THE IMPRESSIONISTS IN LONDON
In 1905, at the Grafton Galleries in London (right), Paul Durand-Ruel held "the greatest Impressionism exhibition ever to have been organized" – as the art historian, John Rewald, described it. There were 55 works by Monet (of which eight are shown in this picture, with three Renoirs); 38 by Eugène Boudin; 19 by Edouard Manet; 59 by Auguste Renoir; 49 by Camille Pissarro; 37 by Alfred Sisley; 13 by Berthe Morisot; 35 by Edgar Degas; and 10 by Paul Cézanne. Considering that all these paintings were part of Durand Ruel's unsold stock, the show indicates the impressive scale of his commitment and investment since the 1870s. Even though all the pictures were for sale, not a single work was sold during the exhibition.

Decorative supplier's label

ALICE WRITES TO HER DAUGHTERS
During a brief round trip to Madrid in 1904, Alice sent Blanche this card from the Prado, and Germaine this letter from Biarritz.

HOLIDAY SNAPSHOT
Here Monet and Alice play at being tourists in St. Mark's Square, Venice, in 1908. "We were both so happy during our visit," he wrote. "She was so proud of my zeal."

A SOLITARY SKETCH
Monet used only one page in this sketchbook from Venice. Similar views of a palace appear in several paintings.

EXHIBITION OF PAINTINGS

BY

CLAUDE MONET

FROM FEBRUARY 1ST TO FEBRUARY 16TH, 1915

DURAND-RUEL GALLERIES

12 EAST 57TH STREET

NEW YORK

SUCCESS IN THE STATES *above*
Monet's status as an international celebrity was largely due to his popularity in America.

GONDOLAS IN VENICE
1908; 80.5 x 54.5 cm (31¾ x 21½ in)
Monet was enraptured by the unique light of Venice. Unable to face returning there after Alice's death in 1911 (p. 53), he worked on his Venice canvases at Giverny: "But it is difficult. I don't stop thinking about her as I paint".

Monet in London

Today's view of the River Thames from the Savoy Hotel

"WITHOUT FOG, London would not be a beautiful city," Monet once said. He had painted views of the misty River Thames in 1870, and returned in 1899 and in the winter months of the following two years. From his room at the Savoy Hotel, he could see Waterloo Bridge to his left, and Charing Cross Bridge and the Houses of Parliament to his right. Across the river, from Saint Thomas's Hospital, he gained a more direct view of the Gothic landmark, which he transformed into an eerie silhouette veiled in a "mysterious cloak" of coloured mists (opposite). Painting this series proved exasperating – the mists changed so rapidly that Monet found himself "feverishly" shuffling through the 100 canvases that he had under way, in search of the one that most resembled the new effect.

RAIN, STEAM, AND SPEED – THE GREAT WESTERN RAILWAY
J.M.W. Turner; 1844; 91 x 122 cm (35¾ x 48 in)
Monet revered the English artist, Turner – though he once denied it. Turner was the most distinguished painter of atmospheric landscape in the l9th century, and Monet knew that the earlier artist's work would be the standard against which his own London images would be judged. This is one of the few paintings that he ever admitted to having studied closely.

London, Houses of Parliament

1904; 81 x 92 cm (32 x 36¼ in)
After his months in London in 1901, Monet decided to take his canvases back home to Giverny to complete the series. "I'm bringing them all along together, or at least some of them," he told Paul Durand-Ruel in 1903, indicating that he finished such pictures in the studio, while referring to others in the group.
News of this working method exploded the myth of Monet painting exclusively from nature, and he was understandably sensitive about it. He commented: "Whether my cathedral views, or my London views ... are painted from life or not is nobody's business, and is of no importance ... It's the result that counts". In 1904, he showed 37 of his Thames pictures, all with descriptive titles. This one was subtitled *Glimpse of Sun in the Fog*.

CHARING CROSS BRIDGE, SMOKE IN THE FOG: IMPRESSION
1902; 73 x 92 cm (28¾ x 36¼ in)
Like Turner's *Rain, Steam, and Speed* (above), this painting enshrouds the dark, linear forms of a railway bridge and steam train in an atmospheric *enveloppe* of fog. The railway motif echoes Monet's early compositions at Gare Saint-Lazare and Argenteuil (pp. 26–27), which combined an interest in modern-life themes with the steam-laden atmosphere of a station. But this time his concern for the *enveloppe* – "the same light everywhere", as he described it – dominates the picture. "To me," he wrote in 1895, "the motif itself is an insignificant factor. What I want to reproduce is what exists between the motif and me". What exists here is the thick London fog, which Monet has depicted as an almost tangible veil of air.

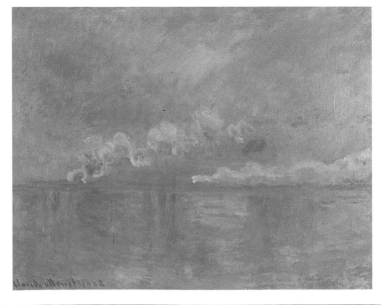

BELATED DATE *above*
Although Monet began work on the *Houses of Parliament* series in 1900, he signed and dated the canvases in this group in 1903 or 1904, when he considered them finished enough for exhibition.

BRILLIANT SUNBURST
The brooding, dark, bluish shape of the building emerges out of the murky, blue river, while subtle nuances of red, mauve, and gold swirl in a flame-like vortex around the canvas. And a fiery red-gold sunset burns a brilliant, widening path across the rippling water of the River Thames.

DRIFTING MIST
The horizontal, wispy flicks of paint with which Monet has painted the river move diagonally and vertically into the towers. They create a sense of distortion and echo the effect of drifting mist.

CLOUDED IN MYSTERY
With the sun setting behind, and veils of mist all around, the Houses of Parliament appear as a muffled silhouette. The painting is suggestive and mysterious rather than simply descriptive. Such poetic evocations were especially praised by Symbolists, including Monet's friend, the poet Stéphane Mallarmé.

51

The garden at Giverny

A Giverny waterlily

WHEREVER HE SETTLED, Monet created gardens and painted them. But it was at Giverny, where he lived from 1883 until the end of his life, that he had the time – and eventually the money – to develop his own floral universe. He favoured densely packed clusters of bright flowers: blossoms cascaded over bowers, spread across gravel paths, and blazed in the crowded borders. "My garden is slow work, pursued by love," he once said, "... I dug, planted, and weeded it myself; in the evening the children watered". After 1890, when he purchased the house, he took on six full-time gardeners to help him. In 1892, he bought a swampy piece of land next to his property to transform it into an oriental water garden "for the pleasure of the eye, and for motifs to paint". Despite local resistance, he diverted the tiny River Ru to create a pond and planted its banks with willow trees, alders, irises, and bamboos; the surface he covered with exotic waterlilies. The pond became the focus of his life and his art for more than 25 years.

AMONG THE GLADIOLI

Monet began transforming the sparsely planted garden as soon as he moved to Giverny, removing hedges, planting lawns and ornamental trees, and creating a richly colourful series of flower-beds. Even when the task became too time-consuming to manage without full-time help, he supervized his team of gardeners closely, giving daily directives to the head gardener. Monet was understandably proud of his beloved garden, and would delight in showing it off to visitors.

THE ARTIST'S GARDEN AT GIVERNY

1900; 81 x 92 cm (32 x 36¼ in)

Designed with a painter's eye, Monet's garden at Giverny was a work of art in itself, as well as the subject of more than 500 pictures. The sheer abundance of his flower garden can be seen in this painting. Although the garden was laid out with flower-beds intersected by gravel paths, Monet insisted that the beds be filled to overflowing to soften the lines of the formal layout.

"What I need most are flowers, always, always," Monet enthused. Here gloriously rich banks of mauve iris lead up to the green-shuttered house, which can be glimpsed through the foliage. The garden is seen in dappled sunlight – trees cast shadows on the gravel paths and create patches of blue among the mauve flowers.

Sprays of lilies line the bank, as seen in the picture on the right

In the pond's mirror-like surface, the reflections create images of perfect symmetry

REFLECTIONS IN THE WATER *above*
Monet was fascinated by water as a motif. Its ever-changing reflections presented "the most fugitive effects" of nature for him to capture. By creating his waterlily pond, he was able to exert control over his motif, arranging the plants around its shore and on its surface.

WATERLILIES
1914–17; 130 x 150 cm (51 x 59 in)
In many of his water landscapes, Monet removed both shoreline and horizon, and here he has created an apparently inverted image. Reflections of lily leaves and clouds pass through the pond's waterlily-dotted surface.

(Above) Monet by the Japanese bridge; (below) the water garden today

Wives and daughters

In 1911, Monet became a widower for the second time when Alice died. He was devastated. More sadness soon followed: after a long illness, Jean Monet died in 1914. His widow, Blanche (Monet's step-daughter and daughter-in-law) devoted herself to looking after the ageing artist.

Monet and Alice chatting in the garden

A VIEW OF THE BRIDGE
Compared with the overwhelming exuberance of the flower garden, which was laid out on formal European lines, Monet's water garden was cool, tranquil and inspired by Japan. Within a relatively small area, Monet created the illusion of space with sinuous curves and picturesque vistas.

SUPPORTING ROLE
Monet's "blue angel" was how Georges Clemenceau described Blanche. She was the artist's constant companion and assistant, and here she is seen ready to pass him another canvas as he works by the pond. In the foreground is Monet's step-granddaughter.

PAINTING UMBRELLA
Blanche was a talented artist herself, who worked very much in Monet's style, but she gave up her own painting to look after Monet. She stayed on at Giverny after his death. This painting umbrella from Giverny may well be hers.

A Japanese bridge

THE DELICATELY ARCHED wooden footbridge was built at Giverny when Monet first created his water garden in 1893 (pp. 52–53). But the plants took some years to grow, and it was not until 1899 that Monet began to concentrate on painting the bridge – it appeared in the first of his *Waterlilies* series. These pictures, with their simple, symmetrical compositions, represent a perfect synthesis of the decorative and naturalistic aspects of Monet's art.

Wisteria

HIROSHIGE'S BRIDGE
Both the bridge and Monet's paintings of it reflect his admiration of Japan. This print (c.1856–59) by Ando Hiroshige shows a similar bridge.

The Waterlily Pond

1899; 89 x 92 cm (34¾ x 36¼ in)

This is one of 18 views of the Japanese bridge that Monet painted during 1899. Like others in the series, it is painted on a squarish canvas and characterized by the bridge's symmetrical positioning. The bridge itself is a sharply "drawn" linear structure, which forms an unbroken curve from one side of the canvas to the other, emphasizing the picture plane. In contrast, the pond's shimmering surface is painted with complex, broken brushwork and creates an illusion of depth.

THE JAPANESE BRIDGE
1918–24; 89 x 100 cm (35 x 39¼ in)
Monet produced this powerful painting when his eyesight was under threat, about 20 years after *The Waterlily Pond* (opposite). Wild, expressive strokes of garish red and gold replace the early work's tranquil, contemplative beauty and naturalistic, cool blues and greens. Not surprisingly, paintings such as this have been regarded as precursors of Abstract Expressionism.

INVISIBLE SKY
In his late works, Monet increasingly limited the field of vision. Here he has blocked out the sky with the dense plants and foliage behind the bridge, and omitted the shore in the foreground. Such works lack the points of reference that are traditionally found in "landscapes", and look forward to abstract art.

WISTERIA TRELLIS
Four years after Monet painted this image, he added a trellis over the bridge and draped it with wisteria, as in Hiroshige's print (opposite). This photograph of Monet and Georges Clemenceau shows how the wisteria softened the stark lines of the bridge.

BANDS OF BLOSSOMS
The pond's surface is defined by the clusters of pastel-coloured lily blossoms. They form a series of receding horizontal bands that are cut through by the vertical reflections of the weeping willows. The composition is tied together by this play between the horizontal and vertical, which echoes the tension Monet has established between the picture's flat surface and the illusion of depth.

Mirror image

MONET'S LILY POND was a constant source of inspiration. He said: "The basic element of the motif is the mirror of water, which changes its appearance every moment". A passing cloud, a breeze, or a change in the light "unnoticed by the untrained eye" transformed the pond for him. The moods of his waterlily paintings vary greatly: some are pale and delicate, while others, such as the picture below, contain an aggressive sense of energy.

REFLECTIONS
As the weeping-willow leaves brush the water, they become almost indistinguishable from their reflections.

Waterlilies

1916–19; 200 x 180 cm (78¾ x 70¾ in)
This large canvas was executed at the water's edge. The paint is applied thinly and rapidly, and the composition is slashed in half by the dark, vertical band of willow leaves. The trail of leaves passing through the surface of the water creates a dynamic tension – it negates the sense of receding space implied by the way the lily pads become smaller and bluer. Only the green triangle of bank in the bottom left-hand corner of the canvas provides a visual reference point.

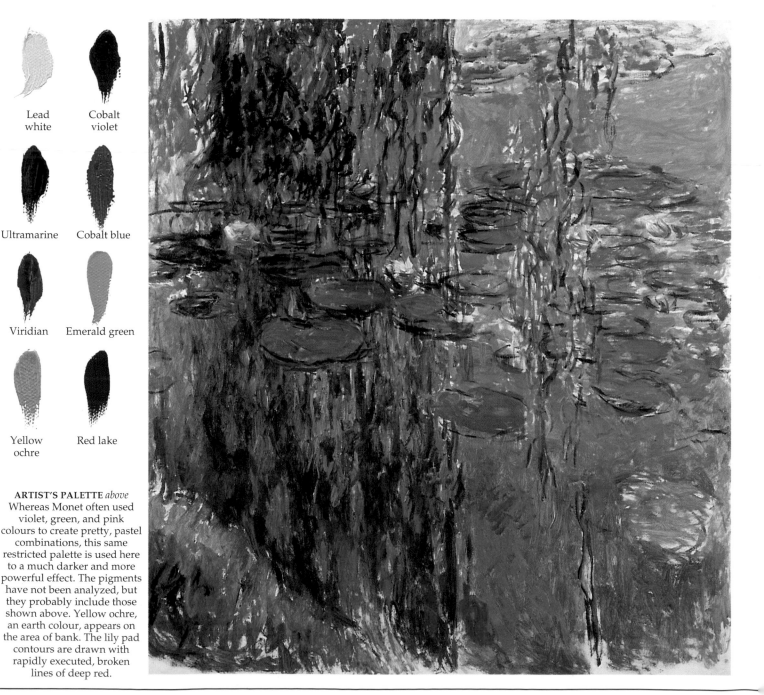

Lead white

Cobalt violet

Ultramarine

Cobalt blue

Viridian

Emerald green

Yellow ochre

Red lake

ARTIST'S PALETTE *above*
Whereas Monet often used violet, green, and pink colours to create pretty, pastel combinations, this same restricted palette is used here to a much darker and more powerful effect. The pigments have not been analyzed, but they probably include those shown above. Yellow ochre, an earth colour, appears on the area of bank. The lily pad contours are drawn with rapidly executed, broken lines of deep red.

PINK AND WHITE BLOSSOM *left*
Loading a wide brush, Monet painted the open lily blossoms with just a few strokes. The bright white and intense violet-pink stand out against the cooler blues and greens, even though the "background" blue has been painted over the edges of the white petals.

Blue water daubed over green leaves

Lily pad contour

A dark flick of paint streaks across the flower

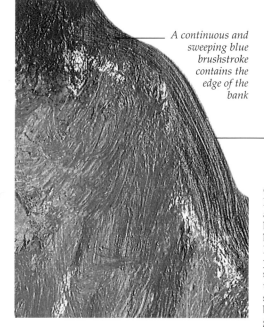

A continuous and sweeping blue brushstroke contains the edge of the bank

ON THE BANK *left*
Monet often included a triangular corner of bank in his water-based compositions. Rough scribbles of yellow ochre and shades of green depict the grassy bank. The spatial relationship between water and ground is deliberately ambiguous.

Flat lily pads contrast with the vertical leaves

Brighter blue "highlights"

A brush has been loaded with unmixed yellow and green paint

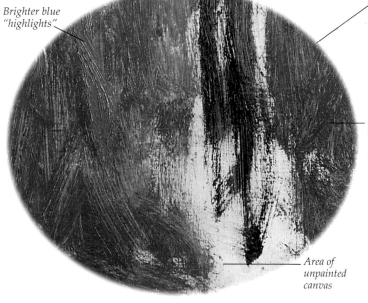

Thinly applied scrubs of mauve

Area of unpainted canvas

RESERVE CANVAS *left*
Monet left a "reserve" of unpainted canvas for the isolated willow trail, to maximize its effectiveness against the pale ground. The green leaves pass over violet water and dangle just above the bottom of the canvas.

REFLECTED LEAVES *above*
As the weeping willow touches the pond's surface, its leaves and their reflections form a continuous feathery trail. Monet did not paint the water first and then the leaves; in the controlled chaos of this passage, mauve, violet, and blue paint passes over and under the green-yellow streaks.

Monet's final years

THE FINAL YEARS OF MONET'S LIFE were fraught with loss – of his wife, his son, and of his own eyesight. And yet during this period he created one of the most magnificent monuments of painting – the waterlily murals (pp. 60–61). After Alice's death in 1911, he rarely left Giverny, but received many visitors at the house, including his dear friend, Georges Clemenceau. As a newspaper proprietor, Clemenceau had been a champion of Monet's work. During the First World War, he was the French Prime Minister, and on Armistice Day, Monet wrote to him saying that he wished to celebrate Peace by giving France two of the huge waterlily decorations on which he had been working. Under Clemenceau's encouragement, the initial, rather modest suggestion grew into a project that would obsess, exasperate, and inspire the artist until his death in 1926.

CONSIDERING THE LILIES *above*
"Caporal" cigarette in mouth, his brush and palette in hand, Monet contemplates one of his waterlily paintings on his 80th birthday. The two-metre (6-ft) high canvases were mounted on mobile easels, which could be pushed together. Monet often despaired of his work, and he destroyed many of these paintings.

MONET'S LATE PALETTE
From the 1860s, when he abandoned dark pigments, Monet made a point of restricting his palette to a limited number of pure colours: mostly lead white, cadmium yellow, vermilion, red lake, cobalt blue, and emerald green. When Monet's colour vision became distorted, he selected his pigments by relying on the tube labels, and on the invariable order in which he set out the paints on his palette.

Thickly encrusted yellow and white

Edge of palette cut off

A FAVOURITE PAINTBRUSH
The hard-edged *taches* – colour patches – of Monet's early work were made with flat, square-ended brushes. As the surface texture of his pictures became increasingly complex and integrated, he used brushes of a variety of shapes and sizes, and had ones with especially long, flexible handles made to order. This well-used brush belonged to him – its large size suited the broad, sweeping strokes of his late work (pp. 56–57; 60–61).

Area covered by thumb is left free of paint

THE LARGE STUDIO
As war raged on the Western front and distant cannon-fire was occasionally heard at Giverny, Monet created a haven of peace with his waterlily murals. The canvases were so big that he had to build a vast new studio (above) to work in.

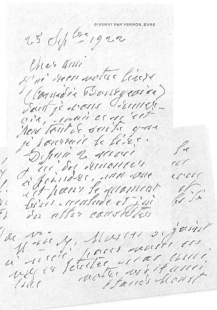

LATE SKETCHES
Monet's sketchbooks contain rough drawings of the waterlily pond that were obviously executed in his final years. Some, such as this one, are drawn in mauve crayon, with broad, loose strokes that seem to reflect both the monumental scale of his late paintings, and his decreased ability to distinguish detail.

"The Eye" goes blind

Paul Cézanne once said of Monet that he was "only an eye. But God, what an eye!". Monet always had "a horror of theories", and he believed that we only really understand the world through our vision, rather than our intellect. His painting was founded on his powers of observation, which became finer and more discriminating over the years. But in 1908, at the age of 68, he began to lose his sight, and he was virtually blind by 1923. Eventually, special glasses and two operations on his right eye by his Paris eye doctor, Dr. Coutela, restored his vision.

Curved, green lens for the "good" eye

Flat, opaque glass for the blind eye

A FRAGILE HAND
Although he could hardly see, Monet managed to keep up his correspondence. In this letter to his friend and biographer, Gustave Geffroy, written in a frail and spidery hand on 25 September 1922, he refers to the cataract operation that is the only chance of saving his eyesight.

CORRECTIVE SPECTACLES
Only one of Monet's eyes was operable; the other was "absolutely lost", as he told Gustave Geffroy. And even after surgery, his perception of colour was both variable and distorted. But in 1925, Monet was prescribed a special pair of Zeiss spectacles (above): "I see colours much better, and can work with more confidence," he wrote.

AFTER THE OPERATION *left*
Here Monet convalesces after cataract operations in 1923. By the time his sight began to fail, two of his old colleagues, the artists Edgar Degas and Mary Cassatt, had already gone blind. He was convinced that a similar fate awaited him. The threat of coming blindness created a sense of urgency, and often despair, as he struggled to finish the waterlily project. During this time, Monet grew increasingly frail, and eventually his doctors diagnosed severe lung disease, which was exacerbated by years of smoking.

BURIAL AT GIVERNY
Monet died at Giverny on 5 December 1926, aged 86. He was not religious, and loved the sea so much that he had once said he wanted to be buried in a buoy. He was interred, without prayers, in the churchyard at Giverny, having outlived most of his friends. Clemenceau is seen here leading the mourners.

Waterlily decorations

THE ARTIST IN BRONZE
This bust of Monet with an intent gaze stands near the murals.

"IMAGINE A CIRCULAR ROOM ... covered with water that is dotted with plants ... alternately green and mauve, the peace and quiet of the still waters reflecting these expanses of blossoms." This is how the essayist, Maurice Guillemot, described Monet's plans for "a decoration" based upon his waterlily pond in 1898. However, 30 years passed before Monet's vision became a reality. The huge paintings that he created are far removed from the small and rapidly executed canvases of his "Impressionist" years. Yet his earlier preoccupations are still evident: water, reflections, and the *enveloppe* – that intangible veil of air that he dedicated his life to painting.

INFLUENTIAL FRIEND
Opposite the bust of Monet in the Orangerie, Paris, is one of his collaborator and friend, Georges Clemenceau, which is sculpted by Auguste Rodin.

Clouds

1926; 1 m 97 cm x 12 m 71 cm (6 ft 5½ in x 41 ft 9 in)

ADJOINING PANELS
All the long panels in the Orangerie are composed of several canvases. One of the joins is just visible above.

Morning, with Weeping Willows

1926; 1 m 97 cm x 12 m 75 cm (6 ft 5½ in x 41 ft 10½ in)

A FRINGE OF LEAVES
The cropped trunks and the trail of willow leaves hanging from the top of the panel accentuate the frieze-like effect.

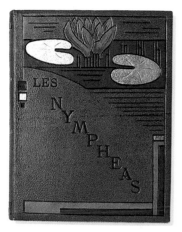

COMMEMORATIVE BOOK
This little book by Clemenceau, entitled *Les Nymphéas (The Waterlilies)*, is on display in the Orangerie. Its stylized cover echoes the decorative qualities of the murals.

"THE SISTINE CHAPEL OF IMPRESSIONISM"
Monet's original idea was to give two of his paintings to the State. But Clemenceau and Gustave Geffroy had a more dramatic project in mind – installing Monet's waterlily canvases in a space of his choosing, creating a vast, decorative monument dedicated to the glory of France.

Years of negotiations and bureaucratic wrangling ensued, exacerbated by Monet's concerns about his failing sight and by his insecurities about the quality of his work. He missed his deadlines and threatened to abandon the project altogether. But in 1927 – the year after his death – the canvases were installed in two oval rooms in the Orangerie.

REFLECTIONS
The reflections of passing clouds on the mirror-like surface of his "enchanted pond" had always fascinated Monet.

SHADOWY CORNERS
In describing the influences on these paintings, Monet referred to the Japanese aesthetic "that evokes presence by means of a shadow", as shown here.

NO HORIZONS
Monet painted the water with neither horizon nor shore, creating "the illusion of an endless whole".

DREAM-LIKE SPACE
Within the panels, space has a dream-like ambiguity. Here the surface of the water appears almost draped behind the weeping willow's trunk.

Key biographical dates

1840 Oscar-Claude Monet born in Paris, 14 November.

1845 Family moves to Le Havre.

1856–8 Selling caricatures locally. Meets Eugène Boudin.

1857 Mother dies.

1859 Allowed to go to Paris, to Académie Suisse; meets Camille Pissarro.

1861 Conscripted. To Algeria.

1862 Convalescing from typhoid at Le Havre. Paints with Boudin and Jongkind. Joins Gleyre's studio in Paris. Fellow-students are Frédéric Bazille, Auguste Renoir, and Alfred Sisley.

1864 Gleyre's studio closes. Monet and friends paint in open air in the Forest of Fontainebleau.

1865 Works at Chailly on *Le Déjeuner sur l'Herbe*.

1866 Paints *Woman in a Green Dress* – a success at the Salon.

1867 First son, Jean, born.

1869 Paints at La Grenouillère, near Paris, with Renoir.

1870 Marries Camille. His aunt dies. Franco-Prussian war declared. Bazille killed in action. Monet flees to London. Meets Paul Durand-Ruel.

1871 Father dies. Monet moves to Argenteuil, on the Seine, near Paris.

1874 First Impressionist exhibition.

1876 Shows at second Impressionist exhibition. Works at château of Ernest and Alice Hoschedé.

1877 Works at Gare Saint-Lazare. Shows at third Impressionist exhibition.

1878 Second son, Michel, born. Family moves to Vétheuil, with Alice Hoschedé and her children.

1879 Shows at fourth Impressionist exhibition. Camille dies.

1880 Submits to Salon and is accepted; has solo show at offices of *La Vie Moderne* magazine.

1881 Moves to Poissy with Alice and children.

1882 Shows at seventh Impressionist exhibition. Paints at Pourville.

1883 Paints at Etretat. Solo show at Durand-Ruel's. Moves to Giverny.

1884 Paints on French Riviera.

1885 Shows at International Exhibition at Georges Petit's. Paints at Giverny and Etretat.

1886 Doesn't show at the eighth and final Impressionist exhibition. Exhibits with "Les XX" group in Brussels, and in New York. Paints in Holland, Etretat, Belle-Ile.

1888 Paints on Riviera. Solo show at Boussod & Valadon.

1889 Paints in Creuse Valley. Major joint retrospective with Rodin.

1890 Buys house at Giverny. Works on *Grainstacks* and *Poplars* series.

1891 *Grainstacks* show at Durand-Ruel's a huge success. Ernest Hoschedé dies.

1892 Begins *Rouen Cathedral* series. Marries Alice.

1895 Visits Norway. *Cathedral* series a triumph.

1896 Revisits Normandy coast. Begins *Morning on the Seine* series.

1899 Monet paints waterlily pond and Japanese bridge at Giverny; begins London series. Step-daughter, Suzanne, dies.

1900 Paints in London and Vétheuil. An accident causes temporary loss of sight.

1901 Paints in London.

1905 Huge Impressionist show at Grafton Galleries, London.

1908 Eyesight starts to fail. Visits Venice with Alice. Works on waterlily paintings in studio.

1911 Alice dies.

1912 Monet completes Venice pictures from memory. Double cataracts diagnosed.

1914 Begins the huge waterlily decorations. Son, Jean, dies.

1918 Offers two large waterlily paintings to the State to celebrate Armistice Day; this evolves into the waterlily murals project.

1922 Almost blind; unable to work.

1923 Partially restored eyesight; resumes painting.

1926 Monet dies at Giverny, 5 December, aged 86.

1927 Waterlily murals inaugurated in the Orangerie.

Monet and Alice in Saint Mark's Square, Venice, in 1908

Monet collections

The following shows the locations of museums and galleries around the world that own three or more Monet paintings.

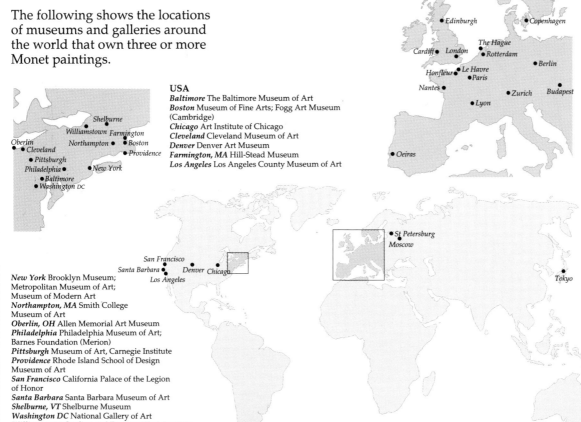

USA
Baltimore The Baltimore Museum of Art
Boston Museum of Fine Arts; Fogg Art Museum (Cambridge)
Chicago Art Institute of Chicago
Cleveland Cleveland Museum of Art
Denver Denver Art Museum
Farmington, MA Hill-Stead Museum
Los Angeles Los Angeles County Museum of Art
New York Brooklyn Museum; Metropolitan Museum of Art; Museum of Modern Art
Northampton, MA Smith College Museum of Art
Oberlin, OH Allen Memorial Art Museum
Philadelphia Philadelphia Museum of Art; Barnes Foundation (Merion)
Pittsburgh Museum of Art, Carnegie Institute
Providence Rhode Island School of Design Museum of Art
San Francisco California Palace of the Legion of Honor
Santa Barbara Santa Barbara Museum of Art
Shelburne, VT Shelburne Museum
Washington DC National Gallery of Art
Williamstown Sterling and Francine Clark Institute

EUROPE

Denmark
Copenhagen Ny Carlsberg Glyptotek; Ordrupgaardsamlingen

France
Honfleur Musée Eugène Boudin
Le Havre Nouveau Musée des Beaux-Arts, André Malraux
Lyon Musée des Beaux-Arts
Nantes Musée des Beaux-Arts
Paris Musée Marmottan; Musée du Louvre; Musée d'Orsay; Musée de l'Orangerie

Germany
Berlin Neve Nationalgalerie

Hungary
Budapest Magyar Nemzeti Muzeum

Netherlands
The Hague Haats Gemeentemuseum
Rotterdam Boymans-van Beuningen Museum

Portugal
Oeiras Fundacao Calouste Gulbenkian

Russian Federation
Moscow Pushkin Museum
St Petersburg Hermitage

Switzerland
Zurich Kunsthaus; Stiftung Sammlung E.G. Buhrle

UK
Cardiff National Museum of Wales
Edinburgh National Gallery of Scotland
London Courtauld Institute Galleries; National Gallery; Tate Gallery

ASIA

Japan
Tokyo Bridgestone Museum of Art; National Museum of Western Art

Glossary

Academic art Art that conformed to the standards of the French Academy, the official body that promoted traditional art based on classical ideals.

Alla prima (Italian: "at first".) A picture painted entirely wet-in-wet, usually, but not necessarily, at one sitting.

Atelier (French: "studio".) Both a teaching studio and an artist's working space.

Broken colour Paint that is not blended together, but is applied in mosaic-like patches, or dragged across a rough canvas or underpaint so that it covers it irregularly.

Chiaroscuro (Italian: "light dark".) The use of light and shade to model form and create an illusion of depth.

Complementary colours Two colours are "complementary" if they combine to complete the spectrum. So the complementary of each primary colour – red, blue, and yellow – is the combination of the other two. Red and green; blue and orange; and yellow and violet are the basic

Broken colour

pairs. In painting, placing complementary colours next to each other makes both appear brighter and more vibrant.

Cool colours The more blue in a colour, the "cooler" it is said to be. Cool colours appear to recede; warm colours, containing larger amounts of red, appear to advance.

Drying oils Oils that harden on exposure to air, and in which ground pigment is suspended to create oil paint: traditionally linseed, walnut, and poppy seed oil.

Earth colours Red- and yellow-browns such as ochres, siennas, and umbers, which are naturally occurring iron-oxide pigments.

Enveloppe Monet's term for the atmospheric "envelope" of coloured light in which a scene is bathed at any given moment.

Flat colour An unmodelled area of colour – an evenly applied, unvaried expanse of red, for example.

Ground The layer or layers of primer applied to the canvas to prepare it for painting.

History painting Paintings depicting historical, literary, legendary or Biblical scenes, intended to be morally uplifting.

Impasto Paint applied in thick, raised strokes.

Medium The drying oil, and the oil or turpentine used by an artist to alter the consistency of paint. Also the material – oil or pastel, for example – with which a picture is executed.

Motif The particular subject of a painting.

Naturalistic Art that represents objects as they are observed.

Palette Both the flat surface on which an artist sets out and mixes paints, and the range of pigments used in painting.

Pastel A coloured stick of powdered pigment mixed with just enough gum to bind the particles.

Pictorial space The illusion of space created in a painting, which appears to exist behind the surface of the picture.

Picture plane The plane in the imaginary space of a painting that is occupied by the actual surface of the picture.

Plein air **painting** (French: "open air".) Painting out of doors.

Pochade A very free and rapidly executed sketch.

Raking light Light cast on a picture at a very low angle, to reveal the textural details.

Realism The French art movement, led by Gustave Courbet, that rejected traditional lofty themes in favour of unidealized paintings of ordinary people and objects.

Reserve An area of the picture surface kept free of paint in anticipation of a later addition.

Salon The official annual art exhibition in Paris, first established in 1667 by the French Academy.

Tache (French: "spot".) A distinctly defined patch of colour.

Reserve partially covered with grey paint

Still life A painting of inanimate objects such as flowers or fruit, often arranged on a table or in some kind of domestic setting.

Warm colours (see **Cool colours**).

Wet-in-wet The application of one colour into or next to another, before the first is dry.

Yellow and blue painted wet-in-wet

Monet works on show

The following is a list of the galleries and museums that exhibit the paintings and pastels by Monet that are reproduced in this book.

Unless otherwise stated, all the paintings in this book are oil on canvas.

Key: t = top b = bottom c = centre
l = left r = right

Index

Acknowledgements

PICTURE CREDITS

Every effort has been made to trace the copyright holders and we apologize in advance for any unintentional omissions. We would be pleased to insert the appropriate acknowledgement in any subsequent edition of this publication.

Key:
t: top *b*: bottom *c*: centre *l*: left *r*: right

Abbreviations:
BN: Bibliothèque Nationale, Paris **BL**: British Library **JMT**: Jean-Marie Toulgouat **JLC**: Jean-Loup Charmet **MHG**: Monet's Home and Garden at Giverny **MM**: Musée Marmottan, Paris **MO** Musée d'Orsay **NGL**: Reproduced by courtesy of the Trustees, National Gallery, London **O**: Orangerie, Paris **PP**: © Collection Philippe Piguet **RMN**: Réunion des Musées Nationaux **RV**: © Roger-Viollet **TG**: Tate Gallery, London

p1: MM p2: *tl*, *mr*: MO; *cl*: RV; *bl*: MM; *br*: Replica of Monet's floating studio, built for the Société d'Economie Mixte d'Argenteuil-Bezons by the Charpentiers de Marine du Guip, en L'Ile-aux-Moines (Morbihan), for Monet's 150th anniversary p3: *tl*: MHG; *c*, *bl*, *br*: MM p4: *tr*: MM; *cl*: JMT; *tl*, *cr*, *bl*: MHG; *br*: Galerie Malingue, Paris p5: Orangerie, Paris p6: *c*: MM; *bl*: Musée Eugène Boudin, Honfleur; *br*: BN p7: *tl*: The Metropolitan Museum of Art, New York, purchased with special contributions and purchase funds given or bequeathed by friends of the Museum, 1967; *bl*: NGL; *br*: MM p8: *tl*: MHG; *tr*: MM; *b*: MM p9: MO p10: *tl*: Lefranc &

Bourgeois, Le Mans; *cl*: NGL; *c*: JLC; *cr*: NGL; *b*: MO p11: *tr*: TG; *cl*, *c*, *bl*: Lefranc & Bourgeois, Le Mans; *cr*: MM; *br*: MO p12: *l*: MO; *r*: MO p13: *tr*: Pushkin Museum, Moscow/Giraudon; *bl*: MO; *cr*: JLC; *br*: Musée Carnavalet, Paris/JLC p14: *tl*, *cr*: Mary Evans Picture Library, London; *br*: MO p15: *tl*: NGL; *cl*: Winterthur, Switzerland/Bridgeman Art Library; *bl*: MO/Bridgeman Art Library; *c*: Letter to Bazille 1869, © The Pierpont Morgan Library,1992, New York; *br*: restricted gift of Mr. and Mrs. Frank H. Woods in memory of Mrs. Edward Harris-Brewer, 1962, 336 photograph ©1992, The Art Institute of Chicago. All Rights Reserved p16: *cl*: MM pp16–17: MM p17: *tl*: NGL p18–19: NGL p20: *tl*: Egarteles Collection, Giverny, France; *tr*: Musée de Vieil Argenteuil, France; *c*: MO; *bl*: MM; *br*: MM p20-21: see p2 p21: *tl*: Musée de Vieil Argenteuil; *tr*: MO; *b*: Medici Collection; *br*: MM p22: *tl*: MHG; *c*: Bayerische Staatsgemäldesammlungen, Munich/Bridgeman Art Library, London; *b*: MM p22–23: O p23: *cr*: photography Roger Brulée; *b*: MM p24: *tl*: BN; *tr*: JLC; *c*: BN; *b*: MM p25: *tl*: Kunsthalle, Bremen, Germany/Giraudon; *tr*: BN; *c*: Musée Carnavalet, Paris/Jean-Loup Charmet; *bl*: MO; *b*: BN; *br*: Archives Durand-Ruel, Paris p26: *tl*: Medici Collection; *cl*: MM; *b*: MM pp26–27: NGL; p27: *tr*, *bl*, *br*: NGL p28: *tr*: Photo by A. Greiner, Amsterdam 1871, Private Collection; *cl*, *c*, *cr*, *bl*: JMT; *cr*: MO/Scala pp28–29: MM p29: *t*: MO/RMN; *cl*, *cr*, *br*: MM p30: *tl*: MM; *cr*: © The Pierpont Morgan Library 1992; *bl*: Municipal Archives of Argenteuil; *bl*: National Gallery of Art, Washington, Collection of Mr. and Mrs. Paul Mellon; *br*: MM p31: MO p32–33: MO p34: *tl*, *bl*: JMT; *cl*, *cr*, *br*: MHG p35: *tl*, *cl*, *br*: Archives Durand-Ruel, Paris; *tr*: MM; *cr*: MHG; *bl*: MM;

cb: Catalogue cover for Monet/Rodin exhibition, Galerie Georges Petit 1889, Bruno Jarret photographer, ©ADAGP, Paris and DACS, London 1992 p36: *t*, *c*: MM; *b*: MHG pp36–37: MM p38: *c*: Archives Durand-Ruel, Paris; *bl*: MM; *br*: JMT p39: *tl*: City of Aberdeen Art Gallery and Museums Collection, Scotland; *tr*: MM; *c*: Courtauld Institute Galleries, London; *bl*: MO; *br*: MM p40: *tl*: Susan Griggs Agency Ltd, London; *cl*: Private collection (as reproduced in *Monet* by Robert Gordon and Andrew Forge, Harry N. Abrams, Inc., 1983); *c*: MM; *b*: RMN, Paris p41: The Metropolitan Museum of Art, New York, Bequest of Lizzie P. Bliss, 1931 p 42: *tl*: JMT; *cl*: MM; *cr*: National Galleries of Scotland, Edinburgh; *b*: MO p43: *tl*: The Trustees of the British Museum; *tr*: The Royal Academy of Arts, London; *cl*: TG; *cr*: National Galleries of Scotland, Edinburgh; *bl*: MO; *bc*: Archives Durand-Ruel, Paris; *br*: British Library, London p44: *tl*: Photo N/D, R-V: *tr*, *br*: MM; *bl*: MO p 45: *tl*, *tr*, *bl*, *br*: MM pp46-47: MM p48: *tl*: PP; *tr*: The Savoy, London; *cr*: MM; *b*: Archives Durand-Ruel, Paris p 49: *tl*: MM; *tc* (top letter), *tr*: BN; *tc* (bottom letter): JMT; *br*: Musée des Beaux Arts, Nantes, France/Giraudon p50: *tl*: The Savoy, London; *c*: NGL; *b*: MM pp50–51: MO p52: *c*: JMT; *b*: MO p53: *tl*, *bl*, *br*: MHG; *tr*: MM; *cl*: RV; *cr*: JMT; *cb*: PG p54: *tl*: Jacqui Hurst *cl*: The Trustees of the British Museum; *b*: MM pp54-55: NGL p56: *tl*: MHG pp56–57: MM p58: *tl*: RV; *bl*: Galerie Malingue, Paris; *br*: MM p59: *tl*: O; *tr*, *cl*: MM; *cr*: © The Pierpont Morgan Library 1992; *bl*: PP; *br*: RV p60–61: O p62: *tr*: PP p63: *t*: NGL (detail); *l*: NGL (detail); *r*: NGL (detail); **Front Cover**: Clockwise from top left: MHG; MM; MO; O, Paris; MM; MM; MO; RV; *c*: MO

Inside front flap: *t*: MM; *c*, *b*: MHG **Back Cover**: Clockwise from top left: MM; MHG; MM; MM; JMT; O, Paris; MM; MM; MM
Additional picture research: Caroline Lucas

Dorling Kindersley would like to thank: Jean-Marie Toulgouat for his kind help in supplying information and photographs. Also, Philippe Piguet for providing photographs. Susanna Price for location photography; Alex Saunderson for additional photography; and Tim Ridley at the DK studio. Thanks also to Luisa Caruso, Caroline Juler and Lol Henderson for their editorial assistance. **Maps:** James Mills-Hicks.

Author's Acknowledgements: First of all, I would like to thank M. Arnaud d'Hauterives and Mme. Caroline Genet of the Musée Marmottan; Mme. Caroline Godfroy and Mme. Frances Daguet at the Archives Durand-Ruel; M. Maurice Medici and Mlle. Isabelle Chretien at Argenteuil Town Hall; M. Troupeau of the Musée de Vieil Argenteuil; Mrs. Lindsay and the staff at Giverny; M. Daniel Wildenstein; John House of the Courtauld Institute for his advice; Ian Chilvers for the invaluable loans from his library; Nick Mutimear for his comments on Etretat; and to David Edgar for advice on Monet's eye condition (and also for his support). I'd also like to thank Susanna Price and Kate Magson, who made the photographic sessions in France such a pleasure. The Eyewitness Art team at DK deserve special thanks: in particular Gwen Edmonds, Laura Harper and Tracy Hambleton, with whom I have worked most closely. Finally, thanks go to my grandmother, whose love of art first inspired mine. I dedicate this book to her memory.